The New York Subway Hero: My Battle with Evil...

and a Spree Killer!!

Joseph J. Lozito

The New York Subway Hero: My Battle with Evil...and a Spree-Killer!!

ISBN:-10: 1499215800
ISBN-13: 978-1499215809
Cover photo by Marcus Santos/New York Daily News
Cover photo design by Joseph J. Lozito

All interior images courtesy of author unless otherwise noted

To my beautiful wife Andrea and my two wonderful sons Joseph and Dominic, it was you that I fought for that fateful day. It is you I will spend the rest of my life fighting for. You are my world. You are my everything. Nobody was going to take me away from you. I love you always.

To Alfred Douglas, you are the hero. Even if I am the only one who has said it, we both know the truth. I will always be grateful for your selfless acts on the only day we've ever met. Heaven holds a special place for you Alfred. Please don't ever change. Without you, the truth may have died with me on the train.

One Thing Before You Begin........

I would like to make something very clear before you read any further. There is a misconception on the part of some that I am anti-cop or anti-NYPD. I am neither. What you are about to read is not an indictment of the NYPD in general. I would say that if you are reading this book and are a member of the NYPD, if you put your heart and soul into your job, if you legitimately put your life on the line daily, the actions that you are about to read should make you sick. I will continue to have respect for anyone who puts on the badge and wants to make a difference. I will continue to have zero respect if you're on the job solely for benefits and a pension. If you are one of those cops who does care and one of those cops who puts forth an honest effort every day, I salute you. Thank you for your service. This story is not about you.

PREFACE

February 12, 2011 was the day I died. Not in the conventional way. There wasn't a priest brought in to read me my last rites nor was I "bagged and tagged". But make no mistake, I died that day. The person that left Philadelphia early that Saturday morning may have had the same body as the person who returned several days later, but what's on the inside and what's upstairs....now *that* was completely different. Many of us have often wondered what's it's like to die. Now imagine that *plus* the added dimension of dying in front of people who not only refuse to help but are willing to watch you die. It's bone chilling.

It's been said that "life can change in an instant" and I know that to be true. Mine is a cautionary tale. Take nothing for granted for it, or maybe even you, may not be there the next time.

Love is an amazing thing. Love is what drove me to fight that day. The love I have for my children, Joseph and Dominic and for my wife Andrea. I've often wondered how hard I may have fought had I had nobody to fight for? Thankfully, I'll never need to know the answer.

What you are about to read is the story of that life-changing day and the ensuing battles that have followed for years, all of which have made me stronger. I have overcome my fair share of turmoil and maybe my story can serve as inspiration for others when they feel as if there is no hope or solution. I consider myself, in the words of Lou Gehrig "the luckiest man on the face of the earth". I have no business writing this book since I have no business being alive. Since I am here though, I plan on taking you through the full range of every emotion you're capable of. I plan on this book being my final statement on the matter so this is it, in full detail for the world to hopefully read and to learn from.

Do not feel sorry for me. Instead, please gain strength from my battles and know that even in your darkest hour, you are capable of extraordinary things.

Understand that while I was "victimized" by Maksim Gelman, while I was "victimized" by the NYPD and later by Corporation Counsel, I do not consider myself a "victim". There is a difference.

Finally, I will leave you with a quote from one of the greatest actors of all-time, Clint Eastwood, in his legendary role as "The Outlaw Josey Wales" that seems applicable when dealing with the events of that day; "Are you gonna pull those pistols or whistle Dixie?"

FOREWORD

"The difference between a successful person and others is not a lack of strength, not a lack of knowledge, but rather a lack of will."

- Vince Lombardi

My own words are not sufficient to describe Joe and his actions so I must use another's. Throughout our lives we come in contact with people who tell us what they would do in any particular situation. It is the true man who puts fear and words aside and acts.

Joe Lozito, who I have known since 1990 has never looked for trouble, fame or notoriety. Never sought the spotlight, only tried to live his life with honor. When confronted with a situation where most of us would have cowered, he acted. A coward attacked Joe and many others, for only a coward preys on those weaker or helpless. True strength, strength of purpose, strength of character and strength of will won out that day.

Joe Lozito wears his heart on his sleeve, thinks of others before himself and puts his family before everything. Joe is the perfect example that nice guys don't finish last and that sometimes, they hit back.

"Integrity is doing the right thing, even when no one is watching"
-C.S. Lewis

To my friend and brother Joe.

Dean Ewen

My sister Angela
In a scene that continues to repeat itself to this day, here I am stuffing my face!

CHAPTER ONE

I was born on October 6th, 1970 in Queens, NY, the firstborn son to Carl and Rosalie Lozito. My parents would later give me a sister Angela and a few years after that, a brother named Carl. My father was born in Italy and came to this country as a little boy & my mother was born in New York. We were just an average, middle-class family living in Middle Village. We lived on 75th Place which was a typical block for the time. All the fathers worked, some multiple jobs while the mothers stayed home and raised the children. From one end of the block to the other, everyone knew everyone and we all looked out for one another. It's very different from a lot of neighborhoods today. To be honest, I've been living in the house I'm living in now for well over a year and I've never met my neighbors on either side of me or across the street. It's just a different time now I guess.

It was a fun block for a kid to grow up on. There were plenty of kids of all ages and we were right down the block from Juniper Park which had something for everybody. Playgrounds, baseball fields, tennis courts, racquetball courts, and tons of hills for us to ride our bikes. Most of us had Ross Apollo Racers which was THE bike at the time. I was one of the younger kids on the block so I guess I had plenty of "big brothers".

We lived in a small apartment downstairs from my grandparents. Basically the garage and the basement were made into an apartment. When I think about it now, the place had to be tiny, but I didn't know any better at the time and honestly, I didn't care. It was "home" and that's all I needed.

I was a fat, geeky (or "husky" as in the size pants my mother would buy me in Alexander's department store every year before school started) comic book and sports nut. I loved Marvel and D.C. comics. I couldn't get enough. My favorite was always Batman. I think I liked his look and the fact that he didn't have any super-powers like the others, but no matter the villain and no matter the peril he was facing in that issue, he always ended up the victor when all was said and done.

Even more than comics, I LOVED sports and if I had my choice, baseball would have been a year-round sport. Even though I could only watch them when they played the Mets or when they were on the NBC Saturday Game of the Week, I loved the Atlanta Braves and Dale Murphy was my hero. Remember, this was way before Al Gore invented the internet so I got all my news by going upstairs and reading my grandparents New York Daily News. Every now and then, they'd run a picture of a Braves player and that was usually the highlight of that day. I'd cut it out and save it. I know I have still a book somewhere with cut-out Braves pictures and articles from the Daily News and New York Post. Every night during the season, I'd watch Channel 11 news and wait for Jerry Girard to give me the Braves score. Thinking about him now, Girard was way ahead of his time as a sportscaster.

I also loved football and hockey. My football team was and is the Buffalo Bills. I honestly don't remember why. My guess is that my Uncle Joe (who lived upstairs with my grandparents) was a Jets fan and loved Joe Namath. The Bills had their own Joe at quarterback at the time, Mr. Joe Ferguson and he was "my guy". My hockey team was, as it is now, the New York Islanders. Most people on our block were Rangers fans, but I went for the Islanders. To me, Bryan Trottier was the best in the game (remember, I was a kid. At that time, he was better than Gretzky... in my mind) and they also had three guys who I thought were the scariest guys in the game in Garry Howatt, Bob Nystrom and Clark Gillies. Howatt was scary because he was smaller than most of the guys but played like he was ten feet tall and took on anybody. Nystrom was just pure physical, raw energy and after he scored the goal to beat the Flyers to win that first Stanley Cup, he was elevated to god-like status to us kids…and probably most adults too. But on my small black and white television, Clark Gillies was the baddest dude on skates. Grown men were afraid of him and at that time, it seemed he never lost a fight. He also looked cool with the beard. I was always Gillies in street hockey, minus the beard, intimidation factor and talent!

I always remember the sports debates we'd have in school and although we all loved sports, the only kid who could match me in sports knowledge and trivia was Johnny Nelson. We were neck & neck in our knowledge of baseball and football, but he knew basketball and I couldn't care less about it and Johnny felt the same way about hockey. I remember "flipping" baseball cards in the school yard. It's true; we bought cards and didn't immediately put them into plastic holders. We kept them together with rubber bands and gasp; we even put them in the spokes of our bicycles!! I remember always taking out the Braves before flipping. I couldn't imagine losing a Buzz Capra or Barry Bonnell card and of course, the Dale Murphy cards were never in play. I think most of the time I ended up trading my Yankees cards to the other kids for their Braves cards anyway.

I enjoyed grade school. We were all growing up together and while we were all different, it wasn't the cliquey, popularity contest that high school would be. I never liked "going to school", but once I was there, I was fine. Grammar school and junior high school while living in Middle Village and Maspeth were cool. Again, I grew up with most of these kids so we were friends from a young age.

We moved to Long Island exactly one month before I started high school. I was still fat, err, husky, shy and awkward. Not a great selling point when trying to make friends. My sister on the other hand had about twenty friends by the end of our first night in Levittown. My brother was five at the time and a cute kid, so he really didn't have too much to worry about.

I made some friends but let's be honest, it's never the same as when you're around kids you grew up with. I always felt like an outsider in general and viewed high school as a necessary evil to get to college. I went to exactly one pep rally (and left after about 10 minutes), one "Spirit Day", and exactly zero sporting events or plays or anything. High school to me was a job. I went and did what I had to do but when it was over, I was out of there. No reason to stay any longer than required. There's no doubt my favorite part of high school was graduation day.

I attended St. John's University for parts of a few years. I didn't graduate nor did I get anything resembling a degree. There was a lot of turmoil at home around this time and I basically decided that continuing my education would take a backseat to getting things in order. I don't regret the decision at all as I can honestly say I doubt I really appreciated the whole college experience and the opportunity to learn at such a prestigious University. At this point, I doubt I'd ever try and go back. I feel that window may be closed.

While I was in still in school I got a job at Bruce Bennett Studios, the #1 hockey photographers at the time. I was a photo researcher. It was a great job and I worked with some great people. Of course I wish it paid more but at the time I started, it was a dream job for a hockey fan. However as the years went on, I met Andrea and realized that this was the woman I wanted to marry and start a family with but that wasn't going to be a possibility working at BBS. Fortunately, a few years after we were married, I started working for Fleer Trading Cards based in Mt. Laurel, New Jersey. It meant relocating and leaving our family, but it also meant a fresh start with a higher salary and a lower cost of living. That my friends, equaled children!

Fleer was my absolute favorite job. I was a photo editor, one of three in the department. We had many responsibilities but the main duty was to pick the photos that would be used for the sports cards. An absolute dream job for a sports nut & card collector! I honestly thought I'd be there forever, but it was not to be. The first three to four years I worked there, the company was doing well but the last year or so was hell. The industry was in the tank and all card companies were trying to find the next big thing. To this day, I'm not sure any company has, I just know that Fleer did not. Couple that with poor decision making at the top and we were all given our walking papers in May 2005 on Friday the 13th to be exact. At that point, that was probably the worst day of my life.

I was out of work for three months which at the time, was a lot. This was before the economy crashed and people would kill to be unemployed for *only* three months. We were alone in Philadelphia with our entire family still up in New York. I was looking online and in the papers every day for work. I would have taken a job anywhere if it paid the bills. I just needed to provide for my family. One thing led to another and I found myself working in the box office of Madison Square Garden that September.

Working in a box office is not as easy as it looks. It's not breaking rocks on a 100 degree day, but it's definitely an arduous task on a daily basis. If your ticket seller makes it look easy, it means they're good at their job. Working at MSG, you deal with all kinds of people. The stories I have could fill up a completely separate book and most people probably wouldn't believe them anyway.

The Garden box office is probably like no other. It's an incredibly stressful place when you first start because I honestly don't think anything can prepare you for the sheer volume of different duties one has there. It's definitely a place for the strong-willed and strong-minded. If you can thrive there, you really can thrive anywhere. I am so grateful for the opportunity to start my box office career there as I learned so much about the business from some really great and knowledgeable people. I also made some great friends that I imagine I'll keep in touch with for the rest of my life.

A position became available at the Avery Fisher Hall box office in late 2009 and I was fortunate enough to be recommended to interview for it. When I found out who I was interviewing against, I didn't think I had a shot. One guy was a buddy of mine with way more experience. One woman had been in the business for decades and I was very close with her husband. I really don't remember who the third person was but at the time, it didn't matter because I figured going up against those two, my chances were zero. Fortunately, I must have made an impression and I was offered the position in January of 2010 and I've been there ever since. The job was an upgrade in many ways; the most important was more security. While I worked steady at MSG, I generally only worked ten months out of the year. Once the Rangers and Knicks seasons were over, the "per diem" workers were generally laid off until mid-September when things would get busy again. This made the summers very stressful as I tried to find work in other box offices or I would have to apply for unemployment benefits. Having a "full-time" position at MSG meant you worked year-round and came with more security. I honestly felt at various times I had earned a full-time position there, but one was never offered. The job at AFH was a twelve month position with more security. The added security meant Andrea and I had a big decision to make, do we stay in our adopted city of Philadelphia or do we come back to Long Island? This was not an easy decision.

Beauty and the beast!

CHAPTER TWO

When the job at Fleer came about, we looked for places in both New Jersey and Philadelphia. We both agreed living in Philadelphia would be awesome and I think we ended up with more for our dollar there. Plus, we lived in Northeast Philadelphia which reminded me a lot of Middle Village. We were both scared but excited.

Philadelphia is an amazing city. It really gets a raw deal in the national scope and I think that has a lot to do with the sports fans. They are fanatical. I'll always remember our first weekend in our new place. We went to the market to pick up groceries and I picked up that days Philadelphia Daily News and the Eagles were on the front page with recaps of the game the day before….against the Tennessee Titans…..in the PRESEASON! That was my first lesson as to what kind of sports town Philly is. Coming from the New York metro area, we had two baseball teams, two football teams, three hockey teams and two basketball teams. New York sports fans have many options and fandom is spread out amongst all nine teams. Philadelphia has one team in each sport and *everybody* in Philly is a sports fan. It's actually very cool, even if a small percentage of fans take it to extremes. The reality is ALL cities have screwy fans that go overboard, the ones in Philly just seem to always make national headlines.

Personally, I loved Philadelphia and it will always have a special place in my heart because both Joey & Dominic were born there. We met some really great people when we were there. For the most part, Philly is a hard-working, blue-collar town and I'm totally on board with that.

When I was laid-off from Fleer, I was hoping to find a job in the area. My goal from the day we moved down there was to plant roots and stay there forever. Unfortunately, there weren't many opportunities for me down there which is why I ended up working in New York. Like I said, the job at MSG never came with any security so it was a safer avenue to maintain our residence in Philadelphia based on cost of living. That decision though involved tremendous sacrifice on my part.

The daily commute from Philly to New York is not as uncommon as you'd think. I certainly realized I wasn't the only lunatic crazy enough to do it when you start seeing the same faces on every step of the journey. I'm not going to lie, it was tough. Eight hour days turned into thirteen hour days and twelve hour days seemed like I was meeting myself coming and going. I did it all for my family, the same family I feel like I wasn't there for half the time. My commute was so time-consuming. I missed so much family time that I'll never get back. I always tried to convince myself it was quality over quantity, but the reality is, those hours add up and nothing I can do will ever bring them back.

The added security of the Fisher box office position opened the door to coming back to Long Island. It's a testament to how much I love my family that I'd even consider coming back. When we left, I was done with New York. I hated it and couldn't wait to leave. I vowed I'd never be back. Now, I was seriously considering relocating back to the very place I couldn't wait to leave. I guess that's part of being a parent and a husband.

The cost of living would be way higher so Andrea would have to work full-time. Up until this point, she would work her hours around the boy's school schedules but coming back and the additional costs would mean a full-time job was a must. Fortunately, her sister Holly worked for the same company Andrea worked for when we left and they said they'd interview Andrea for a position which she was eventually offered and subsequently accepted. It was now official; we'd be New Yorkers again.

While it is true that the new job at Avery Fisher Hall coupled with the horrific five hour round trip commute led to our coming back to Long Island, one other little, tiny thing may have played a part in it. It happened on a cold February morning in 2011...you may have heard the story......

I LOVE this picture
of me with my boys!

Chapter Three

Hockey, when played the right way, is a beautiful sport. Part of what makes it beautiful is that although the sport is played by some of the most graceful athletes on the planet, the game itself is played with an element of violence. The game has "settled down" considerably from the "wild west" style of the 1970's, but the fact remains that although the physicality of the sport is a mere fraction of what it used to be, *and what it should be,* the next scuffle or scrap may only be a second away.

On February 2nd, 2011, the Islanders paid a visit to Pittsburgh to play the Penguins. The Islanders quite frankly did not put out their best effort that night, but the game will forever be remembered for a fight between goalies Brent Johnson and Rick DiPietro. The Penguins had the better of the play all night and Johnson played a great game in net. Earlier in the game, Pittsburgh's Maxime Talbot cheapshotted the Islanders Blake Comeau and the tone was set for the evening. Several scrums ensued after whistles all night and Johnson frustrated the Isles with his play. Late in the game, one such scrum ensued in DiPietro's crease initiated by Matt Cooke. Let's call Cooke the accepted term of "agitator". I generally call him other things, but I digress. Isles Zenon Konopka and Matt Martin intervened and the three were penalized and ejected. During the same stoppage in play Johnson and DiPietro ended up battling and Johnson laid out the Isles goalie. The arena erupted as did the Penguin bench. The most animated Pen was goalie Marc-Andre

Fleury. The loss did not sit well with the Islanders and this set the stage for what fans like me like to call a "revenge game".

The Penguins were scheduled to visit the Nassau Coliseum nine days later. I absolutely had that game circled on the calendar. The Isles had their warriors dressed that evening and what transpired in Pittsburgh was not going to be repeated. In a nutshell, the Islanders slapped around Pittsburgh both on the scoreboard and on the ice. Players like Trevor Gillies, Michael Haley, Martin and Konopka led the charge with physical play and the Islanders rang up nine goals on the aforementioned Johnson and his smiling sidekick Fleury. The Penguins were a better team, but not on that night. It was gut-check time for the Islanders and they answered the bell every time it rang…and rang a few bells of their own in the process.

Why am I telling you all this? Because I was raised on this style of hockey. The style I refer to as "the right way" to play the game. The style that has all but been eliminated from the game today. It was a Friday night and I had to work the next day, but who cares? I watched the NHL Network for hours just for the highlights and interviews from the game. The next thing I know, it's around 1:30-2:00 in the morning. Normally, this isn't a big deal. My Saturday schedule had me starting after 12:00 noon anyway, but as a favor to a co-worker, I switched hours and my new start time was now 9:30 AM. I knew I'd only be working on a few hours sleep but it didn't matter. This game had me amped up. I couldn't wait to get to work and talk about it. The ironic thing was, none of my co-workers are really big hockey fans but truth be told, I would have talked about this game to an army of mannequins!

My alarm went off before 6 AM on February 12th, 2011 and I had to get ready for work. It's amazing how you can look at the same thing in two different situations and have opposite opinions of it. As I left my house that morning, my 2 ½ hour commute from Philadelphia to New York City awaited me. I loathed the commute. Hated it with a passion, but you do what you have to do to support your family. I was a little more tolerant of the 2 ½ hour commute home for obvious reasons. Little did I know that I wouldn't see home until a week later.

My commute started in Philadelphia, generally with a stop at Wawa to pick up a Philadelphia Daily News, a cup of the finest decaf in all the land and an egg white and turkey sausage "sizzli". *Man I miss Wawa.* Then I hit the road with a drive north into New Jersey's Hamilton Train Station where I would usually pick up a copy of the New York Post. Armed with my Philly Daily News and my New York Post, I'd be brought up to speed with the news in both cities by the time we hit Newark. This particular day however, the Hamilton Station Dunkin Donuts hadn't opened yet so my commute continued without the Post.

I figured it was for the best. After all, I hadn't slept that much the night before. Saturday papers are the thinnest of the week. I could finish the Philly paper by New Brunswick and catch a quick nap. While my recollection is fuzzy about exactly how long it took me to read the paper, the nap was a definite. I woke up somewhere between Newark and Secaucus, wiped the sandman out of my eyes and waited to arrive at New York Penn Station.

I envision hell to resemble Penn Station. Millions of people love New York and all that comes with it. I am not amongst that group of people. Penn Station during rush hour is just an absolutely awful place. The only word I can use to describe how I feel about Penn Station is "abhor". I abhor Penn Station, especially during either rush hour.

Penn Station early on a winter Saturday morning is a completely different animal. You have people like me who still have to get to work, but you also have several people without homes looking to escape the cold. You have several people who have homes but thought it'd be a good idea to stay out all night finally making their way back. You also have the usual riff-raff that accompanies any train station in a large city.

What you also get at Penn Station on Saturdays and Sundays is plenty of delays and/or cancellations on subways due to construction. For those not familiar with the New York subway system, it's probably a lot like the rail system in your area (if applicable). It has several lines going all over the city running both local and express routes. The train I take to work is the #1 train, a local train that makes all stops. My stop is 66th street, Lincoln Center. The total travel time is less than 10 minutes. Two express trains run the same route, only they obviously don't make all stops. The #2 and the #3 trains are the express trains that are an option for me. They don't stop at 66th street, but they both stop at the next stop, 72nd street. On a nice day, the six block walk can be rather pleasant.

This particular morning, there was construction on the tracks utilized by the #1 train so all three trains, the #1, #2 and the #3 were all running express. I didn't find out until I had reached the platform for the #1 train. Now I had a decision to make. It's a decision I've had to make numerous times. Do I stay on the platform for the #1 train or do I go around to the platform for the #2 and the #3? Every other time I was faced with this dilemma, I decided to stay on the #1 train platform. For reasons that I still can't explain, on February 12, 2011, I decided to make my way to the other platform and grab the #2 or the #3. Twice as many trains stop at that platform. I figured I'd get to work quicker. It didn't quite work out the way I planned it.

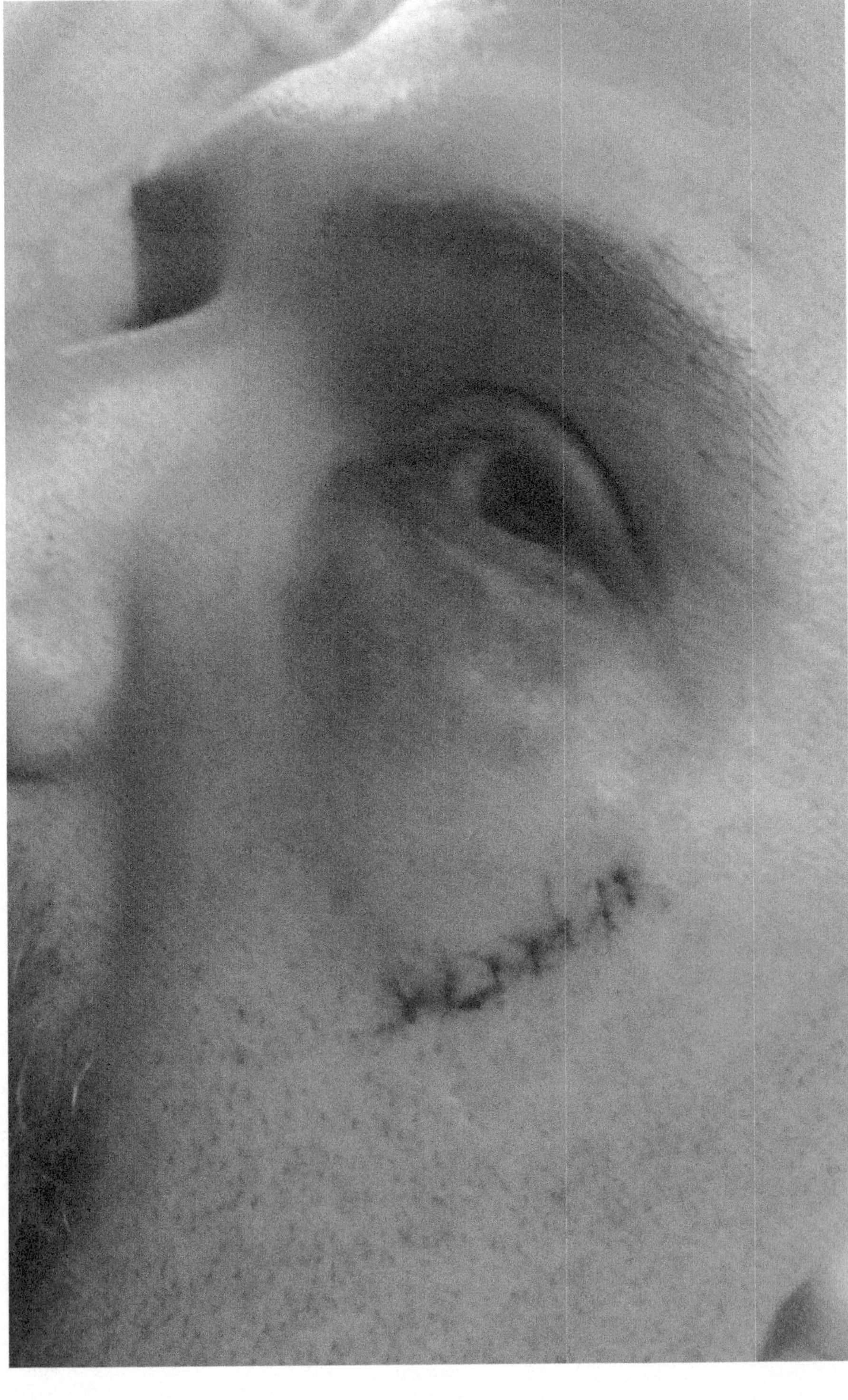

Chapter Four

As I made my way to the opposite platform, there was nothing unusual to alert me of the absolute chaos I'd be a part of mere minutes later. It was just a typical platform on a typical Saturday morning in New York City. People talking to each other. People doing a variety of things on their phones, tablets or various iProducts. People looking down the tunnel to see if the train is approaching. Parents keeping an eye on their kids to make sure they don't go over the dreaded yellow line. Of course you always have the various "entertainers", the singers or musicians who strategically play on the weekends when the city is ripe with tourists who are willing to give them money as part of the "New York Experience" as opposed to the Monday through Friday crowd, most of whom don't pay them a second look on their way to and from work.

My strategy for getting on a train of any kind is simple, walk to either end of the platform. It's been my experience that people will settle near where they emerge from, be it from the stairs, escalator, etc. I've never been one for crowds so I make the walk to one end or the other. These are generally the least crowded parts of the platform. My platform position of choice heading to work is the front of the train. I don't really have any reason for that, it just is.

The first train to arrive that morning was an uptown number #3 train. I entered the train at the front-most set of doors and took a seat on the bench directly behind the engineer. Basically, the only thing separating the engineer and myself was a wall. A few moments later, amongst another group of passengers, two uniformed NYPD officers (one male, one female) entered the train and went directly to the engineers cab. It seemed a bit odd for several reasons. I've been on several trains where officers were going station to station and they'd always stay in the car with the rest of the public. Also, from a practical standpoint, there isn't a great deal of room in the cab portion of the train. To fit three average size people would probably be uncomfortable. I didn't know how big or small the engineer was but I knew that while the female cop was of average size, the male cop was a pretty big man and he was bigger than I was.

Another thing I noticed was the chatter on their radios. The volume seemed like it was turned up full blast and the talking was non-stop. Even after they entered the cab I could still hear their radio's through the door. What was being said I had no idea, but it definitely got my attention. I shrugged it off at that point. I just wanted to get to work and start my day. The quicker the workday starts, the quicker it ends. On top of that, I had a hockey game to talk about with people who couldn't give a crap!

Many times after boarding the subway, I hear this dreaded announcement "ladies and gentlemen, we are being held at a stop signal blah blah blah". I hate that announcement. Just more time I have to sit on the subway, or what I now refer to as "Thunderdome". This Saturday however, there was no such announcement, yet we weren't moving. The train was idle and the doors stayed open and.....*nothing.* I would venture to say that the doors to a subway generally stay open for thirty seconds to a minute from open to close. Now it had been several minutes and we weren't moving. Finally the doors closed and we were on the move.

"Move" in this instance is relative. Yes, we were indeed in motion, but it felt like someone was pushing the entire train from the back car manually. We were moving at the proverbial "snail's pace". Again, I took notice, but what could I do? Out of nowhere, this man walks up to the engineer's door and proceeds to bang on it several times and yells through the window "let me in!" The police, stationed on the other side of the door answer "who are you?" to which the man replied "I'm the police". Common sense would dictate that at some point during the conversation, the officers looked through the window at the alleged cop. Once the man told them that he was the police, the male officer answered "you're not the police". With that, the man turned around and walked towards the other end of the car. Keep in mind, this all happened less than six inches away from me. I remember thinking to myself "what the hell is going on"?

Several things stood out about the man. If he were indeed a cop, he was undercover. He was tall, maybe 6'1" and lanky. He was wearing a coat and he looked dirty. Shady was also a thought that came to mind. A few things made me realize that maybe this gentleman isn't a cop. First, my guess would be protocol would dictate when announcing yourself as a police officer, the displaying of a badge or NYPD identification would be required. Also, the actual cops in the cab told him he wasn't a cop and finally, as he made his way towards the other end of car, he attempted to sit next to a woman but before his ass hit the seat, her ass was out of there!

Just then a man who was standing next to me on my left bolted towards the engineer's door, the same door the first man had just banged on. However this man had a different agenda. He looked terrified and was frantically trying to get the attention of the cops. He was tapping on the window and waving them out, tapping and waving, tapping and waving. Unlike the first man, this man did not receive an answer, but just as the first man couldn't get the cops to open the door and/or come out, the second man was also ignored. At this point, "what the hell" turned to "WHAT THE FUCK!!!!!?"

While the second man was attempting to get the police to leave the confines of the engineer's booth, he was looking over his shoulder to see exactly where the first man was. At some point, the first man started to make his way back to the door and the second man hightailed it back to his original position next to me. While my eyes were fixed on the second man, they quickly switched as I saw the first man making his way back up towards me. As he approached, he stopped about two feet from me, about three feet from the door and reached into his jacket and pulled out an eight inch cooking knife. The next few seconds seemed like slow motion. I saw the blade crystal clear. It was filthy. I thought it was dirt or rust but as I found later it was the blood of earlier victims. He was holding it like he knew how to use it. Holding it with bad intentions. While this part probably took less than two seconds in real time, it seemed like forever. With the knife securely in his hands, evil in his eyes and ill-will in his black heart, the man looked down at me and uttered the words that give me chills to this day..."you're gonna die, you're gonna die"!! Moments earlier, things were in slow motion. Now things sped up exponentially. The second "die" had barely left his lips and before I knew it, he plunged that knife into my left cheek right below my eye. I guess he meant business. However, as President Ronald Reagan once said, "he counted on America to be passive. He counted wrong"

Enjoying a day on the diamond with Joey.

Chapter Five

Chances are, unless you have a Master's Degree in "Badassery", you've never heard of Dean Ewen before reading the foreword of this book. It has been an honor to call Dean my best friend for over two decades. Although Dean was born in Saskatoon, Saskatchewan about a year and a half before I was born in New York, we may as well be twins....or at least brothers. Dean would be the older, better looking, more athletic and more intelligent twin and I'd be, well...not that stuff. I am bigger though, always have been. Only the two of us will get that inside joke, but allow me to continue.

I met Dean during New York Islanders training camp in 1990. Dean was selected by the Islanders in the third round of the 1987 NHL Entry Draft out of the Western Hockey League. If you know anything about the WHL during that time, you know it was full of badasses. Dean was right up there at the top. Plain & simple, this once self-described "impetuous little mutant" was an ass-kicker. He was what is commonly known in hockey circles as an enforcer. Some call him and others that do his job "goons", but they're idiots. He could also play the game. "Goons" generally don't get drafted 55th overall, ahead of such players as Shawn McEachern, Garth Snow, and most notably Theo Fleury.

The long and the short of Dean's career comes down to politics. He was a leader of men and when he had a coach who had confidence in him as a player, he produced. When the coach wanted to use him as a one-dimensional fighter, as many coaches do to enforcers, his numbers to the left of the penalty minute column suffered. Bottom line, I've watched several enforcers play in the NHL during the time Dean played in the minors who were not as tough nor had his skill level, yet they may have received that "break" that Dean never did. Dean never complains about it, it's not his style. That's part of why I respect him so much.

On November 11th, 1993, Dean and I were having a phone conversation, about what specifically, I don't recall. One thing we did talk about was an event that was going to be on pay-per-view the following night. He told me about an organization called the UFC and basically it matched up several disciplines in the martial arts, boxing, kickboxing, and wrestling to determine once and for all who was the toughest and which discipline was the best. Today, it's commonly referred to as "mixed martial arts" but back then it more "no-holds barred" and marketed as "There are NO Rules! ". To say I was intrigued was an understatement. I tuned in the next night and couldn't believe what I watching. Sure, if you compare it to the MMA events of today, it's very primitive but back then, wow! I videotaped that event & watched it so many times; I think I wore the tape out.

Back then, I still watched WWF wrestling and I'm not sure if that had anything to do with this but for some reason, I gravitated towards the "real" wrestlers of the UFC. My first favorite fighter was Dan "The Beast" Severn from Coldwater, Michigan. I don't know why but I can't say his name without telling you where he's from. I also became a fan of fighters such as Mark Coleman and Mark Kerr, all world class wrestlers and during their primes and amongst the elite in the sport.

Myself, I never wrestled. Never in junior high, never in high school nor in college. My wrestling experience pretty much started and ended with me throwing my brother around. I'm nine years his senior so he loved it when I'd fling him all over the place when he was a kid.

The reason why this history lesson is important to the story is that after Gelman stabbed me in the face, as he recoiled his arm back to prepare to stab me again, I instinctively went for a freestyle wrestling move called a single-leg takedown. The general process of a single-leg takedown involves grabbing one of the legs of the opponent, usually with both hands, and using the position to force the opponent to the ground. Typically, the lower part of the leg is pulled in one direction, while the torso or shoulder is used to press the body or upper part of the leg of the opponent in the other direction. Again, I have never wrestled in my life and the only reason I can think of for even attempting this is due to the fact that by that point, I had watched almost two decades worth of MMA. The only problem was, my inexperience with the move almost proved fatal.

When I shot in for his leg, I shot too high and found myself wrapping my arms around Gelman's waist. At this point, it was more like a football tackle than a single-leg attempt. While I was wrapping him up in this tackle, I also gave him free reign at the right side and the back of my head and he did a number on it. I felt his arm moving like a piston digging that blade towards my skull. Each plunge was accompanied by an animalistic grunt. In spite of all that, I was able take him down and in the process, gain dominant position. There were only two problems now-first, I was severely bleeding out and second, he still had the knife.

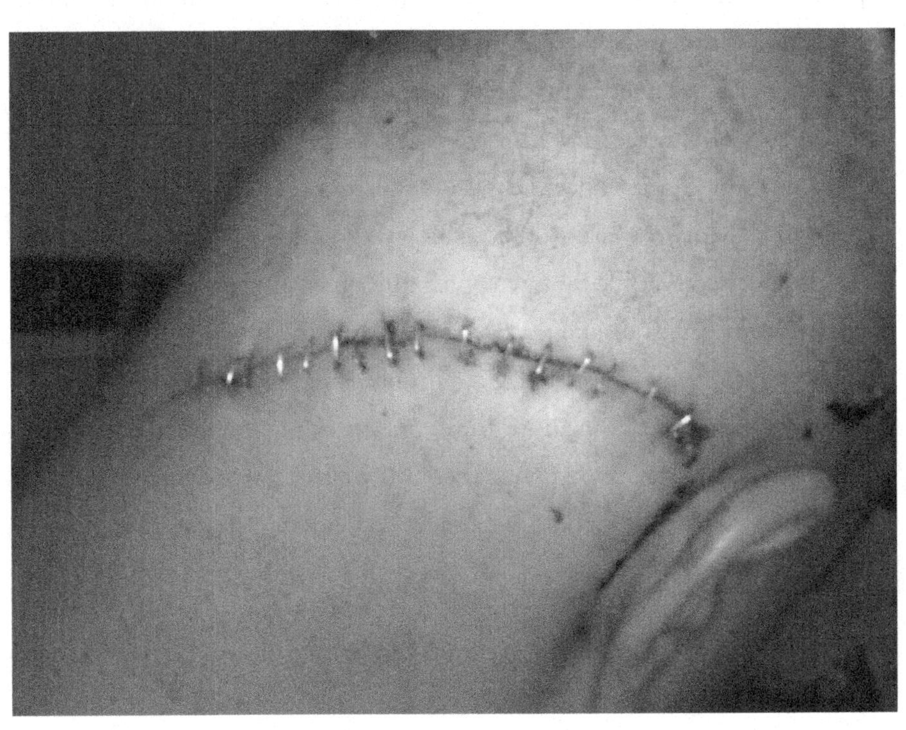

Chapter Six

I had Gelman mounted. I was in dominant position and I'd love to tell you that I wanted to drop some vicious elbows right to his face but I'd be lying. I'll leave that for the two in blue in the engineers cab…but more about that later. At this point, all I wanted to do was separate his hand from that blade.

I don't know exactly what drugs this guy was on, but he was, plain and simple, a killing machine. If someone is reading this to him right now, he's probably got a dumb smile on his face and is rubbing his inner thigh. It's true though, cold-blooded killer with only one mission. Even with being heavily outweighed and absorbing a lot of the blow of me landing on him (my knees took a lot of damage as well); he was still focused on killing me. I saw it in those empty eyes of his.

As he stabbed upward with his right hand, I tried to catch his wrist with my left hand. I missed his wrist, he missed my face but he did manage to slice me in the left thumb down to my tendon. I missed his wrist again with his second stabbing motion but again deflected his arm away from my face. This attempt did slice me in the upper arm however and he sliced me down to the tricep. Finally, on his third attempt to widow my wife, I caught his wrist, stopped the motion and slammed it to the ground with all my power. The knife jumped from his hands and it was now inches away from the scuffle.

It's times like this where a man's character is tested. I'll confess something right now that may be alarming to some. I can say unequivocally that had I been able to grab the knife and use it on Gelman, I would have in a heartbeat. Whether that changes your view or me or not is up to you. Understand that what kept me alive at that moment is that I changed. I was no longer myself. I was the primitive, animal, caveman version of myself. Common sense went out the window. Compassion went way before that. Right then, it was kill or be killed and if I could have grabbed that knife, I would have and I would have done my best to make sure we were BOTH carried out of the subway.

Before any of that could have happened though, I felt a tap on my upper back. It was one of the cops from the cab, Officer Terrance Howell. I get the tap on the back and I hear him say "you can get up now, we got 'em".

I didn't move right away. I had Gelman pinned down with my bodyweight and both hands. For the first time, I had a second to absorb just what was happening. The other cop from the cab, Officer Tamara Taylor made her way to my left side. She kicked the knife away and picked it up. This was honestly the first time that the amount of blood that was pouring out of me registered. I held Gelman down so the larger Howell could mount him and handcuff him, well, attempt to handcuff him.

I stood up and made my way to a subway seat. It was easy to see that most of the passengers that started the trip with me were now either in the next car or way down at the other end. I don't blame them at all. I sat down and watched as Howell struggled to handcuff Gelman. Taylor was no help. Instead of getting down on her hands and knees and aiding her partner, she stood over Gelman and asked Howell if she should mace him to which he replied "no". I put my head down to try and make sense of what was going on but also to try and catch my breath. I needed to be ready just in case Gelman freed himself of Howell. This guy tried to kill me, if he got away, what would stop him from attempting to finish the job? At that moment, I was just overcome with rage. Who is this guy to try and kill me? Who is he to decide that I'll never see my kids again? Who is he to decide that I'll never have another wedding anniversary? No, now I was pissed off and I looked over and just screamed out "YOU BETTER HOPE I FUCKING DIE BECAUSE IF I DON'T, I'M COMING BACK TO KILL YOU!!" Unfortunately, that burst of anger absolutely wiped me out. Had he escaped Howell's grip and come after me, who knows what would have happened? That wasn't a worry for long as a passenger ran over to the scene, got down on his knees and helped Howell handcuff Gelman.

With that bad guy under wraps, you'd think it'd be time to get the train moving and get me to a hospital. To say I was bleeding profusely would in reality be an understatement. I sat and waited for a few moments and figured we'd be moving shortly. I imagined getting medical attention to a guy who was just attacked would be "priority one" for "New York's Finest". As you'll soon find out, that was "hard lesson learned #1". I realized just how unimportant, in the eyes of the police, I was. Oh wait, what's the word I'm looking for.... "expendable"

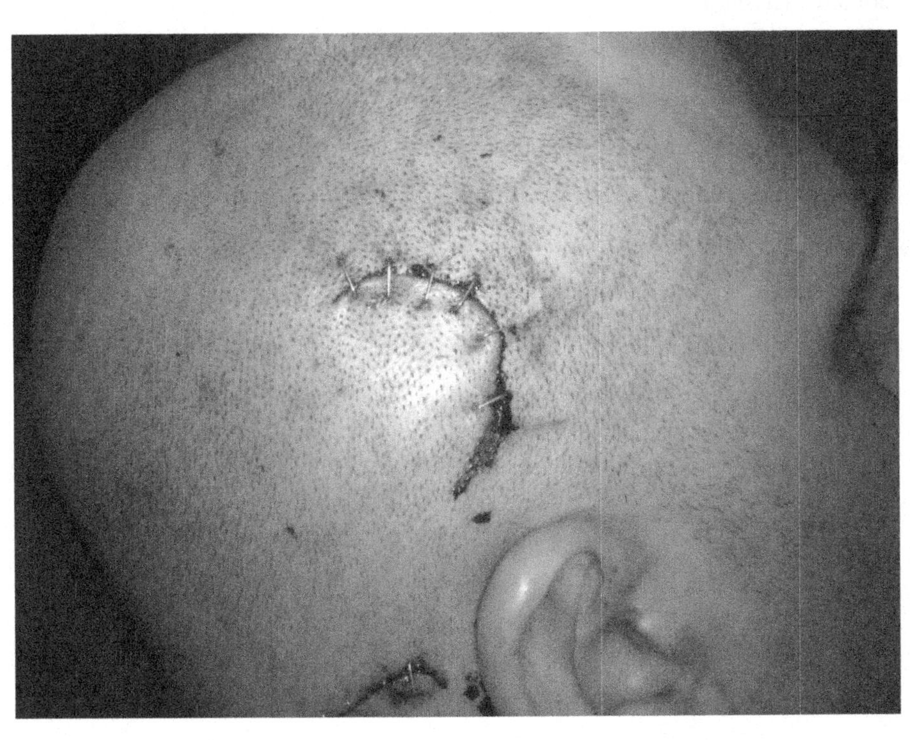

Chapter Seven

Allow me to set the scene for you. We're still aboard the #3 train. We're sitting in the tunnel between 34th street and 42nd street. I was just attacked by Maksim Gelman and despite seven total wounds to both of my hands, my left arm, my face and worst of all, my head, I was able to stifle him with the absolute worst single-leg takedown in the history of mankind….all in clear view of the cops who were on the train specifically to arrest Gelman but must have been distracted by something. Maybe a couple was dancing on the subway platform? Maybe a man was trying to board the subway with a vicious animal like, say a Shih Tzu? If you think I'm lying, do an internet search on those incidents and prepare to shake your head and utter "WTF" in some way, shape, or form. A passenger, not Officer Taylor, has helped Officer Howell handcuff Gelman. I'm sitting on the train and my life is leaving my body via extreme hemorrhaging. Now you're all caught up.

As I'm sitting on the subway seat, Gelman is handcuffed and things appear to be settling down, that is except for the insane amount of blood pouring out of my head. After my outburst where I vowed vengeance against Gelman, I was exhausted. I started telling myself to calm down. I could feel the blood spraying out of my head with every beat my heart was taking. I figured if I got excited, my heart would race and the blood would come out faster. If I calmed down, maybe the flow would slow down. I'm not a doctor so I don't know if any of that was true, but it made sense at the time. It's amazing where the mind will go when you're waiting for the reel of your life to start rolling before your eyes.

As minutes passed, more and more cops entered the car via the back of the train. First, one or two and by the time I was carried off, there had to be six to eight of "New York's Finest" in the car with us. As I impatiently waited for the train to move, on more than one occasion, I yelled out "we need to get this train moving" or "please get me out of here" or something to that effect. Basically, my life was a priority at that point, even if I was the only one who felt that way. The final time I bellowed "can we get this train moving, what's the hold-up?" I was told by an officer that they can't turn the power on because other officers were on the tracks and they'd be in danger. Here *I* am, bleeding-out right before *their* eyes. I was *definitely* in danger, but I guess since I wasn't dressed in blue and wasn't wearing a badge, *I* could wait.

More minutes passed and at some point, the thought crossed my mind that the subway car I boarded at Penn Station could quite possibly be an oversized casket for me. The puddle of blood at my feet was only getting deeper and the only thing preventing me from "drowning" in it was that much of it was being absorbed into my clothes and the backpack that I was still wearing. An officer attempted to walk past me and I reached for their arm. I looked up and said "do you have kids?" and the answer was "yes". I said "I have two sons and they need me and I need them. I can't die on this train. Please, we have to get this train moving". I was reassured, or patronized, that the train would be moving shortly. The clock kept ticking. More time goes by. More blood exits my body and I grab another cop and ask "are you married?" and the reply was "yes". I then begged "so am I. I need my wife. I can't die on this train. Please, when are we going to move? I need a doctor". This officer told me not to worry that paramedics were on their way from the back of the train. I should just keep watching towards the back and they'd be there shortly. I had no reason to doubt the officer at this point. Other officers had made their way to the car via the same route, so why couldn't the paramedics?

At that point, a man, another passenger from the train approached me and applied direct pressure, barehanded, to the deepest wound on my head. This is a man I had never met. He knew nothing about me. He knew nothing about my medical history. He had no idea if I was carrying a disease that could be transmitted by blood. He didn't care. Another human was dying alone right before his eyes and he selflessly and heroically did what he thought was the right thing to do. As he was helping me, he turned to the other passengers and started scolding them, saying "you're all going to watch this man die? None of you are going to do anything to help him?" Another passenger brought him napkins or tissues and he covered part of my wound with them while continuing to apply direct pressure. All the while, I'm still looking towards the back of the train for the medics, yet all I can see are horrified passengers.

At this point, approximately twenty to twenty-five minutes have passed since I stopped Gelman. How I wasn't dead or at least unconscious was beyond me. I know that the passenger, who I later learned was Alfred Douglas, was a huge part of me still being alive. What I also found out later was that the passenger who helped Howell handcuff Gelman was the same Alfred Douglas. Talk about a hero!

An officer at the front of the train yelled out "ok, we're moving, we're moving" and I screamed "WAIT! What about the paramedics? Aren't they on their way?" I was told "they're waiting for you at 42nd street". When I was told the paramedics were coming through the tunnel, that was a boldfaced LIE!

We started moving and we made it 42nd street in no time at all. As we pulled into the station, I could see the paramedics waiting on the platform. At least the police weren't lying to me about *that.* Of course even this couldn't go smoothly as now there was a problem getting the doors opened. This might have been a three or four second delay, but right about now, every second mattered so I admit, I was a little sensitive about it. Finally the medics come in and Alfred stepped aside. I thank God he put Alfred on that train. Not only did he save my life, he allowed me to stand up and tell the truth through this book. I applaud Alfred for his bravery.

The medics tended to my wounds and now they wanted to lift me from the subway bench to the stretcher. My ass isn't an inch off the seat and I pass out. I'd never passed out before and it's truly a remarkable phenomenon. It basically feels like when you nod off watching television. I was unconscious, yet I could still hear everything going on around me. I could hear the medics imploring me to stay with them and just the general chaos of the situation. I could hear the chatter of the cops who were standing behind the stretcher. Amongst the chatter, I heard one of them call me "likely". With that, I snapped out of it and now, for the first time throughout the entire ordeal, I'm feeling pain. It's a pain like I had never felt before. Agonizing, crippling pain is the best way to describe it. I've likened it to dousing my shaved head with gasoline and lighting it on fire. The only positive from the pain was if I could still feel it, I knew I wasn't dead.

Once I was secured on the stretcher, it took four or five officers to carry me up the station steps. I do give them credit for that as that's easier said than done. An officer stationed above ground asked his colleagues "is that the vic or the perp?" On the surface, the question reeks of insensitivity but as I learned later, it's just an example of how inept some members of the force could be. At that point, I didn't know there was a city-wide manhunt for Gelman...*but that officer did.* You'd think the callous officer would have remembered Gelman's face from the picture the police were all shown. Maybe not. Maybe that's too much to ask? I was also greeted with the now commonplace people with their cell-phone cameras snapping away. I guess there are worse things to be photographed for.

I was lifted into the ambulance and the paramedics settled me in and tried to settle me down. I was yammering on about the pain and begging them to keep talking to me. Most of all, I begged them to keep me alive. I don't know who they were, but they could not have been more helpful and courteous. They are definitely in the line of work they're supposed to be in. They took the time to tell me that they can't keep painkillers stocked in the ambulance but not to worry, the staff at Bellevue hospital was waiting for me to arrive and they'd have morphine at the ready. Thankfully, it was a Saturday morning and traffic was at a minimum, even for New York City standards and the ambulance arrived quickly. A member of the staff waited for us at the door. The last thing I remember about the paramedics is that they told the staff about my pain and told them to get morphine in me ASAP.

I was wheeled in rapidly and came to rest in a room not far from the door. It seemed every second brought two or three more people into the room. People were hooking me up to things, tending to wounds, cutting off my clothes, etc. It was even more chaotic than that, but at the same time, I felt a sense of relief because now I was in a stable environment where I could be taken care of. In the midst of it all, a police officer came to the head of my bed and held up a mug-shot. The conversation, verbatim, went as follows:

P.O.-"sir, is this the man who did this you?"

Me-"yes it is"

P.O.-"well then, you're a hero"

Me-"I'm not a hero, why am I a hero?"

P.O.-"because he killed four people last night."

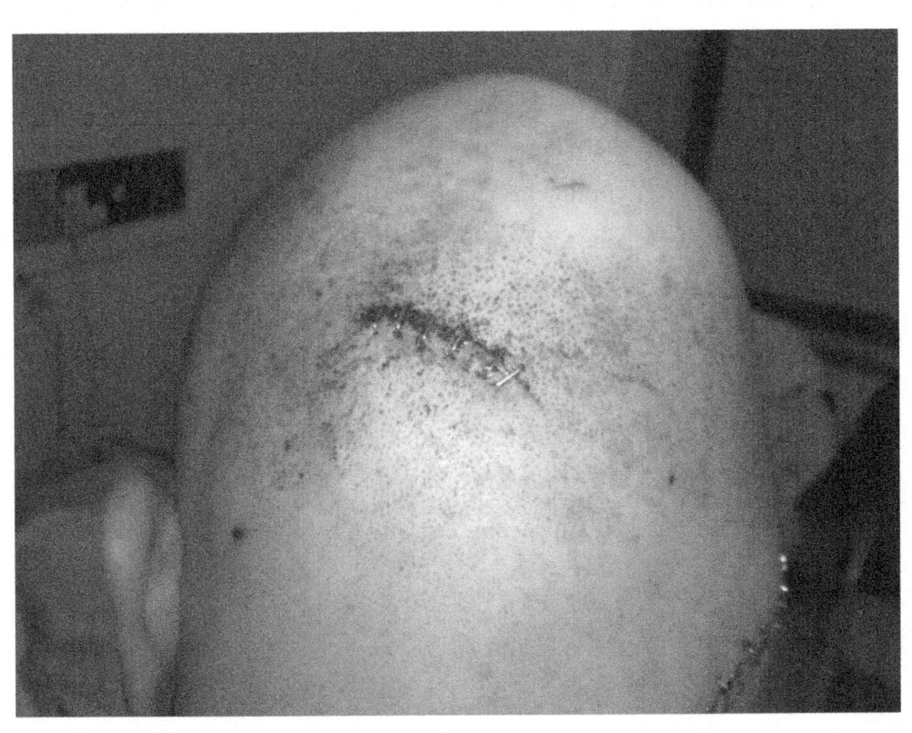

CHAPTER EIGHT

How many times in your life have you been wrestling with your buddies, or play fighting with them and you've said "you're dead" or "I'm gonna kill you"? Probably plenty of times. Obviously you don't mean it. Maksim Gelman and I weren't friends that day and honestly, if we are to become friends, he's got *A LOT* of explaining to do! We may need Dr. Phil and the "That's What Friends Are For" singers serenading us in the background to start building that bridge. It's probably not going to happen, sorry if I got your hopes up.

Maksim Gelman told me I was "gonna die". Even told me a second time for emphasis and he did his best to keep his word. At the time, I figured this was just some random psychopath who was having a bad day. I figured he decided to pick the ugliest guy on train and make him pay for it. It wasn't until I arrived at the hospital and that police officer informed me of his "exploits" the previous twenty-eight hours that I realized I was dealing with a whole different kind of crazy.

To this day, when I tell this story, the part about the officer in the hospital telling me "he killed four people last night" gives me goosebumps. I remember him telling me that and me not being able to say a word. I know I wanted to say something, but the gravity of his words left me dumbfounded. What do you say to that? Fortunately, the chaos of the room diverted my attention, but I just couldn't get those words out of my head. I still can't.

Most of the medical staff at Bellevue hospital was top notch. Most. Once I was stabilized, they took me to another room for X-rays and I believe a CT scan. The staff cared for my head like it was a newborn baby, ever so gentle. They knew what they were dealing with, they could see it. For whatever reason, I never thought to touch my head at any point during this whole ordeal. That was probably for the best. I can't imagine what that would have been like and to this day, I have little desire to feel my own skull.

After that I was wheeled to a room where the doctors were going to put Humpty Dumpty back together again. At this point, the morphine had been flowing for a bit so the pain was reduced to discomfort. Waiting for me in the room were a few detectives who were very cordial and professional. I asked them to call my wife. She was working that day and on Saturdays, she did the books for her job so in order to concentrate on the money, she generally ignored her phone, especially when phone numbers she didn't know appeared. After a few attempts, I asked the detective to give me my phone and I would try to call her. I texted her first which is humorous in and of itself since I think we only added texting to our plan weeks earlier. I finally relented on that one. I admittedly didn't give her enough time to call me when I started calling her. One thing you must know about me, I have a weird sense of humor. Andrea and I started dating in 1992 so she's pretty much seen and heard it all from me. This is why our conversation went something like this:

Me-"hey, there was an incident on the subway. I got attacked by a guy with a knife and I'm at Bellevue".

Andrea-"shut up, you're so stupid".

Me-"no An, I'm serious".

Andrea-"Joe, stop. I don't have time for this. I'm really busy and I don't want to get in trouble for being on the phone".

Me, taking a deep breath and pausing for effect, "Andrea, listen to me, I'm ok, but there really was an incident on the train. I was attacked and I was stabbed several times". With that, even through the phone, I could feel the air being sucked out of her body as I could hear the panic in her voice and I could hear her start crying and screaming. I heard her co-workers rushing in to see what was going on and I felt helpless that I couldn't comfort her. The doctors were ready for me so I told her that a strange number would be calling her in a moment and it would be a detective with further instructions. I hated hanging up that phone. Another detective asked who else they could call and I gave them the number of my mother and my sister. I informed them that my sister was NYPD so I think they may have called her first.

The doctor who repaired my head was awesome. The injection(s) used to numb my head were anything but. They hurt like hell! Once they took effect though, we were all set. The doctor talked me through everything and was very professional. He was going to tend to six of my seven wounds. The wound to my left thumb would have to be seen by a plastic surgeon. All the wounds to my head required both stitches and staples. I had never been stapled before and it was an interesting feeling. My head was numb so I just felt the pressure, but the actual "clicking" of the, for lack of a better word, "staple gun" was a bit jarring.

Once my head was put back together again, the doctor stitched my face and my tricep. Taking a look at a knuckle on my right hand, he told me it was probably a two stitch job and I said just leave it be. He looked at my thumb again and again said it needed to be looked at by a plastic surgeon. At some point, family started rolling in. I don't know who arrived first, but before I knew it, my mother, sister, brother, mother-in-law and sister-in-law were there. I'd never been so happy to see them. My brother was like a caged animal. He wanted a piece of Gelman bad. My brother is a very emotional man and many times, his surroundings are irrelevant. Hospital or not, he was furious and everyone knew it. He probably scared a few people as well.

My sister went off to talk with the detectives for a little bit and eventually she came in to see me. We talked for a little while and one of the things I told her made her turn white as a ghost. As I was recalling the story, I told her about the officer calling me "likely". She froze. She looked at me and said "they called you likely?" and I said yes and she said "Oh my God Joseph, likely means "likely to die"!" Again, what do you say to that?

Seeing my mom was a relief. I was happy she could see me even if was in, as Ferris Bueller would term it, my "weakened condition". I was just glad that all of them could see me bruised and battered, but still alive. The only thing left and the most nerve-wracking part of the episode so far was waiting for Andrea to arrive from Philadelphia with Joey and Dominic. I was getting nervous. I never liked her making that trip without me in the first place under normal circumstances and now she had to drive all the way up here and having no idea exactly where she was going or what she was walking into. I asked my sister to keep watch and wait outside for them.

Before I knew it, I saw Andrea and the boys peek through the curtain. It was glorious. I was so happy to see them. I had probably never smiled that big in my life. I have no idea what any of them had in mind before they got there but I hope my reaction eased much of their anxiety.

I was fortunate that all the extreme damage was done to the side and back of my head so when they walked in, they saw my eye all busted up and the stitches below it, but didn't have a clear view of all the "zippers". They cried and of course I did, hell, I probably started crying first. The reasons I fought to get off that train were all now here. All was right, or at least as right it could possibly be given the circumstances.

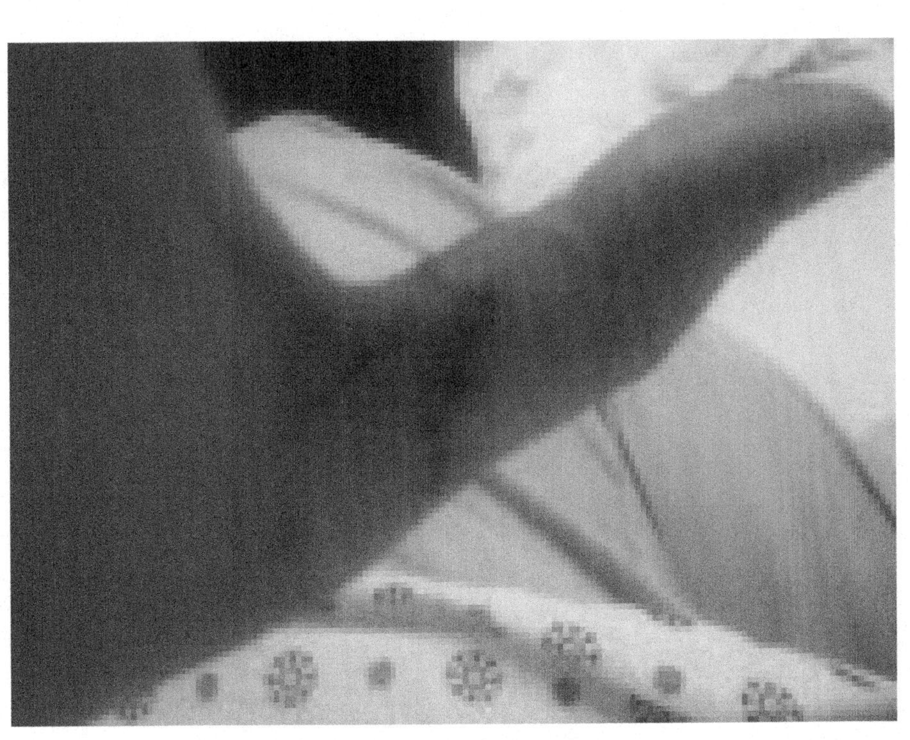

CHAPTER NINE

The last doctor to see me for repairs was the plastic surgeon assigned to assess my thumb. As cool as the doctor who pieced my head back together was, this guy was basically the opposite. He had the bedside manner of Dr. Kevorkian. Sorry about that. I'm pretty sure *everyone* uses Dr. Jack when they're referencing a negative about a doctor, but when you combine the obvious with a simpleton… that's what you get!

The guy was just arrogant beyond belief. He had this way about him from the second he walked in. Just making idle chatter seemed to bother him but the cherry on top was when I asked if I'd be getting a blood transfusion. He looked at me like I was crazy and he said with disdain "blood transfusion? You didn't lose *that much* blood". I know I said, "well, you weren't there" and then he uttered some "I'm a plastic surgeon and you're not" type drivel and I just employed a tactic I use with people when I have no desire to argue with. I said "OK, you're right". I couldn't be bothered with this guy anymore. I just wanted him to tie my thumb back together and then get the hell away from me. I have a very low tolerance for arrogance and this guy had really rubbed me the wrong way.

I was moved to another room where I was still surrounded by my family. By this time I was starting to feel a little more comfortable. Don't get me wrong, the swelling still made it feel like someone inserted bowling balls in my head, but being with people I cared about made things easier. My sister grabbed lunch for me and shortly thereafter, everyone left and I was moved to a more private room with Andrea by my side.

I wanted to call my dad in Kansas so he could hear my voice and know that I was ok. He was very upset and wanted to fly in ASAP but I told him to hang tight since I didn't know how long I'd be in the hospital. My preference was that he'd come for a visit after I was home in Philadelphia anyway. After all that, I listened to the voicemails on my phone. There was an obvious difference in the messages left before the incident and after.

After a while Andrea and I settled in to watch television. I remember we had channel 7 on and they teased highlights from the press conference about Maksim Gelman being arrested, so we didn't change the channel. As the news started, the Gelman arrest was the lead story. As they went to the podium, I saw Mayor Michael Bloomberg and Police Commissioner Ray Kelly amongst others. Then I heard the words that still make me furious, "thanks to the swift action of Officer Terrance Howell and Officer Tamara Taylor, along with off-duty Officer Marcello Razzo, the police apprehended Maksim Gelman on an uptown #3 subway train earlier this morning". I turned my head, Hulk Hogan style so my ear was facing the television better. Surely I missed my name. Could the Mayor be so concerned with Super Big-Gulps or whether newborn mothers breastfeed or used baby formula to have butchered my name so badly? Lozito doesn't sound like Razzo and it definitely doesn't sound like Howell or Taylor. None of us look alike. As Andrea and I waited for him to continue, they finally addressed me. I was not the guy who stopped Maksim Gelman. I was not the guy who helped (I typed with a chuckle) stop Maksim Gelman. No no, none of that. When I was finally acknowledged by the Lords of New York, I was referred to as "Gelman's final victim". Unnamed. Just "victim".

Understand, I wasn't looking for credit, but please don't credit those who did absolutely nothing or those who picked and chose their spots as to not wrinkle their uniforms. Hell, when I saw the picture of Razzo, I didn't even remember him on the train at all. He "allegedly" helped Howell handcuff Gelman. That's funny, because the guy I saw help Howell was named Alfred Douglas. They *look* as much alike as their names *sound* alike....and that's not at all!

I mustered up enough energy to laugh at the whole thing but inside I was pissed. Andrea had no such issues hiding her disgust and neither did my sister when we talked on the phone. My question was why did the officer at the hospital, a man I had never seen before nor ever have a conversation with before, call me a hero upon my arrival? Maybe he didn't get a copy of the script yet? Maybe he was just going off the FACTS available at the moment? I don't know but I hope he wasn't reprimanded for speaking the truth!

As the day turned into night it hit me that I wasn't going to get out in time to attend that evening's Strikeforce card at the Izod Center in New Jersey. Most people wanted to see one of the all-time greats in Fedor Emilianenko as did I, but the two guys I really wanted to see were kickboxing legend Ray Sefo and up & coming Long Island fighter Gian Villante. Villante was from Levittown, NY like me, although he was from the "bad guys" side, the MacArthur Generals. It took me a few days to find out the results and I was disappointed to see both suffered losses. I've been fortunate enough to see Gian fight live twice now and I'm honored to call him a friend. As for Sefo, that was probably my last chance to see the legend fight live, but he lives forever in my K-1 dvd collection.

Sleeping that night was a disaster. I couldn't get comfortable physically and of course every time I closed my eyes, I relived the scene from earlier that morning. I asked for something to help me sleep and I honestly don't remember if I got it. If I did, it didn't help. I was exhausted come Sunday morning and I was absolutely stunned when I was told I'd be going home later that day. I wasn't too disappointed as I wanted to see my boys and the rest of my family, but I figured after what happened, was thirty-six hours really enough recovery time? Welcome to the new world of health insurance.

Post-concert with Dominic

Chapter Ten

I'd say I "woke up" Sunday morning but that would imply that I actually slept. I may have had brief moments of sleep but that was about it. I was surprised when a nurse came in and told me that I'd be going home that day. "Shocked" is a more accurate word. I questioned it and she told me there was nothing more they could do for me. I usually accept reasoning from medical professionals on things, but this didn't make sense. I was still very weak from all the blood loss and my head was pounding beyond belief. At this point, twenty-four hours after the confrontation, psychologically, I was ready to go home. I wanted to hug my kids. I wanted a bear-hug from Joey and a "head-popper" from Dominic. A 'head-popper" is a hug Dom gives me by hugging me as tight as he can around my neck and then instantly releasing it while saying "POP!". They always mean something and every one is like the first. Physically, however, there was no way in hell I should have been released.

I got up to stretch my legs and greeted the officer stationed outside my room. It was a scene that I had done the night before with a different officer. Both were extremely pleasant and had nothing but kind words to say about what I did. They also both asked the same question to which I didn't have an answer, "why didn't they just shoot him?" I replied "I wish I knew".

Before heading back to bed, I knew I had to take a look at myself in the mirror. I hadn't done that yet and honestly, I was a little freaked out. I didn't know what to expect. I wasn't Brad Pitt to begin with so I figured the reflection in the mirror would resemble Dr. Frankenstein's baby boy. I stood in front of the mirror with my eyes closed and when I opened them, it was pretty much what I expected. Cuts, staples, and stitches throughout and my eye was busted up pretty good. I guess when you take down a spree-killer single-handedly; you're bound to suffer some injuries. It was at that point when a harsh reality came over me, now I definitely had no chance of becoming a male model.

At some point in the morning, a reporter from the New York Daily News, Simone Weichselbaum, made her way to my room. She was very polite and courteous and asked if I had a few minutes to talk about what had transpired the previous morning. I agreed and asked where I should start. She said to start from the beginning. As I'm telling the story she's taking notes, nodding, interjecting questions…all the usual reporter stuff. When I finally got to the part about me taking Gelman down, she stopped, looked up at me and said "wait, *YOU* took Gelman down?" and I said "well, yeah". Her reply was "you know, that's not what the cops are saying" to which I simply said "I have no idea what the cops are saying, but this is what really happened". Her eyes lit up as she showed me the Sunday print editions of her paper and the New York Post. As I skimmed the articles I noticed…well, let's call them "inaccuracies" in what the NYPD was stating. Simone asked if I had spoken with any other reporters that day, which I had not. I declined her offer for an exclusive simply because I figured this was news and everyone has a job to do and other reporters might come by. As Simone finished up our interview, she told me the story would be in the Monday print edition but would hit the Daily News website later that day.

Shortly thereafter, another reporter, Amber Sutherland from the New York Post arrived and we had a similar conversation but it was cut short by hospital personnel. I don't know what the issue was. I told them I didn't mind them in my room but they would not relent and forced them out. To this day, I don't know if that's hospital policy or if they were under orders from the NYPD to keep the media out. All I know is they were adamant about getting them out of there.

A little while later my Aunt Maria and my cousin Courtney came to visit and it was so great to see them. They were obviously upset but pleased to see I was in pretty good spirits considering. They told me that my cousin Christian, Courtney's brother, was actually stuck on a subway behind mine for a while due to "police activity" (ironic, isn't it?). He was stuck on the subway and didn't know why. I'm just glad his day didn't start earlier that morning or who knows if he would have run into Gelman. Thank God we never have to worry about that. They also told me a reporter from the New York Times was waiting downstairs and that the hospital would in no way, shape or form let them up to my room. Again, I don't know why, but the Times people patiently waited until I was released.

I was released mid-to-late afternoon on Sunday and did the interview with the Times. Then we were on our way to my mother's house. That would be home base for the next week or so. I guess at some point, Simone's story had hit the internet because all of sudden, my phone was blowing up with all these numbers I didn't know. I started listening to the messages and they were from all kinds of print and electronic media members. It was just so overwhelming. I called my mother to let her know we were on our way and then I just put the phone down, put my head back and rested until we reached our destination.

We arrived at my mother's house and it was awesome. Much of my family was there and it was great to see everybody, but I was exhausted. I rested for a bit then I started returning phone calls. The "Today" show wanted me in studio the next morning, as did "Good Morning America". I called "Today" back first as they were the first to call me, but I never heard back. "GMA" was anxious to have me and they were sending an SUV to pick up Andrea & I the next morning. I figured I'd do the one interview, come back and sleep. At some point that Sunday, our friend Kathleen contacted Fox 29 in Philadelphia to inform them of what happened and told them they should cover it because that was my station of choice. She also informed them that I'm a huge fan of one of their reporters, Steve Keeley. Steve's a pitbull, plain & simple. If I did something wrong, his would be the last face I'd want knocking at my door. If I did something right, I'd want him championing my cause. Apparently they listened. Kathleen is very persuasive. To put it bluntly, she gets shit done!

Channel 7 in New York reached out and wanted to know if I'd talk to them that evening and since they were willing to come out to my mother's place, I said sure. A little while later, Carolina Leid and a cameraman (sorry sir, I don't remember your name) arrived and we shot the piece. I thought it went well. We all gathered around the television at 11 PM for Eyewitness News to watch the finished product and we were pleased.

My phone rang shortly after that with a Philadelphia number. It was Steve Keeley. I have to say, I thought that was pretty cool. He was awesome and told me that after he did his early morning newscast on Monday that he was driving up to New York City to interview me himself. We agreed we'd do it after GMA. Steve was real classy and we talked for a bit. He warned me about what to expect. Never having been in the news, I figured I'd do the GMA piece, do the interview with Steve and head back. Steve warned me that by the time the GMA segment was finished, there would be a swarm of reporters waiting for me. I think he laughed as he said "I don't think you realize how big of a story this is". I told him how honored I was that he'd drive up to interview me and I promised that if he was right about the throngs of media, he would indeed be the first one I spoke to after GMA.

As he usually is, Steve was right. It was a bigger story than I thought and yes, once it got out that I was in Manhattan on GMA, the media was lined up en masse!

With Future Hall of Fame
Catcher Brian McCann

CHAPTER ELEVEN

Working on very little sleep, Andrea and I climbed in to the luxurious SUV that ABC was kind enough to send for us. I don't remember what time it was, but it was EARLY. I was nervous…really nervous. Do you have any idea how many people watch "Good Morning America" every day? Me neither, but I know the number contains several "0's".

We arrived at the studio in what seemed like no time at all and before I knew it, we were behind the scenes of one of the more well-known programs in the history of television. Several ABC staff members greeted us and had wonderful things to say. They treated Andrea and I like royalty. I cannot say enough about it. We met so many people that day it was nuts. I remember one of the producers asking me "are you ok, are you nervous?" and I know I mumbled "yes". She gave me great advice, she said "just listen to Robin". Robin is Robin Roberts. You may have heard of her. Talk about a hero. Talk about someone who is tough. Ms. Roberts took on breast cancer and kicked its ass. If that weren't enough, in 2012, she was diagnosed with myelodysplastic syndrome. She received a bone-marrow transplant and took a leave of absence from GMA. She's back and better than ever. I've been watching her since her days at ESPN but I think she was born to be on GMA. We had a few minutes to talk and she was truly amazing. She could see I was nervous so she grabbed my hand and told me to forget all the cameras, forget all the staff, forget everything around us. Just focus on the conversation with her.

That advice really put me at ease and it's advice I use to this day. We had our talk and honestly, she was amazing. I thought I did ok at best but it looked better on camera than I thought it would when I was doing it. The absolute BEST thing that happened to me in terms of doing interviews with the media was that my first interview was with a true legend and icon, Ms. Robin Roberts. I am forever grateful to her and wish her all the best!

One thing about the piece really bothered me. ABC ran a computer regeneration of the scene on the subway that couldn't have been more incorrect. It had all the players but the positioning was all wrong. They had not consulted with me so I couldn't correct them. From what I've been told, it was created based on what ABC was told by the NYPD. Now it all made sense. In the regeneration, I was sitting in the middle of the car (not where I was ACTUALLY sitting, opposite the motorman), Gelman hadn't attacked me yet and the Officers had already come out of the motorman's cab. We all know that didn't happen. Even the officers know that's not how it happened. At that point, it was too late, but I always remembered that. The propaganda machine started with that press conference and it was continuing.

When we were done with GMA, I hugged Ms. Roberts and thanked her profusely. I called Steve Keeley and as he predicted, there were plenty of reporters waiting for me. I wanted Steve to be the first to speak with me after GMA so we met at a side door and he escorted me to where the Fox 29 van was. Along the way, all the reporters asked for an interview and I assured them I'd get to all of them once I was done with Steve. Truth be told, it was awesome to be interviewed by Steve. I was honored he'd drive up from Philadelphia to interview me in person instead of setting me up at Fox 5 and doing the interview via remote. I've admired him for a long time and Good Day Philadelphia was a morning staple in our house. At certain points during the interview, morning anchors Mike Jerrick and Sheinelle Jones would ask questions and I had a blast. One of things I miss most about not living in Philadelphia anymore is not being able to watch that show.

When Steve and I were done, or when we thought we were done, he received word that "Fox and Friends" wanted to interview me. This was also very cool because one of the hosts is a gentleman named Brian Kilmeade who I first became familiar with when he was part of the early UFC broadcast team. The interview went great except it took me a while to adjust to the delay in his asking the question and me answering. I think I kept stepping on his lines but he made me feel very comfortable. He played a comment WWE Superstar Chris Jericho made about me where he said "if you're a subway slasher, don't attack guys that size, I mean I wouldn't go after that guy". That was pretty awesome, especially coming from a guy like Jericho who'd feed me my lunch in less than five seconds! After that, we went back to talk to Steve, Mike and Sheinelle for a few more minutes and when we were done, Steve and I thanked each other and I remember him saying something that I thought was all class, he said "do these interviews and if that SUV leaves, call me on my cell and I'll personally make sure you guys get back to Long Island". I must say, that was awesome of him.

I went down the line talking to all the reporters while simultaneously keeping an eye on the SUV. I told all the reporters "that's my ride back to Long Island, if he leaves, I leave". Reporters from all of the network's were there and I also remember speaking to a reporter from Inside Edition. By the time it was over, I think we did about ten interviews. I was exhausted and that SUV looked pretty good. I think I sprawled out, took a deep breath and tried to relax.

The whole morning was so overwhelming. Every single member of the media was great to us, but I was so uncomfortable talking about myself. Everyone was calling me a hero but to this day, I don't agree with them. I said it that day and I'll say it now; I did what anyone else would have done. I basically spent most of the interviews deflecting credit to anyone, police, firemen, EMT's, etc. It was easier to do that than to take credit. It's just not my style to talk about myself.

As we made our way back to Long Island, my phone was still blowing up but I was tired and I was only picking it up for family. I got a message from CNN saying that they saw I was in New York City and was hoping I could do a spot in the afternoon. I distinctly remember turning to Andrea and saying with all the energy I could muster "there's no fucking way I'm coming back to the city today". Soon after, Headline News called me with a similar request as CNN had and again, I turned to Andrea and said "there's no fucking way I'm coming back to the city today". I told Andrea I'd return all the calls when we got back to my mother's house and I'd do any interview provided they came out to Long Island or if I could do them over the phone. We held hands & smiled at each other. This certainly was the most eventful Valentine's Day we'd ever had and I absolutely, positively meant what I said, no way in hell I was going back to New York City that day...or so I thought. You know the old saying, "never say never".

CHAPTER TWELVE

When we arrived back at my mother's house, I could think of only one thing, sleep. My mom told me how great I was on GMA (I could have sucked and she still would have thought I was great) and told me how she was saving the other shows on her DVR. While I can't confirm this from memory, I'm sure she asked if I wanted something to eat as she would normally do in any situation. If she did, I declined. I then remember Andrea asking if I would mind if she went upstairs to take a nap and I told her I'd probably be joining her in a little while. First I just needed to check my messages and return some calls. If people still really wanted to interview me, who was I to say no?

I returned calls to CNN and HLN and politely declined their requests to come back to New York City for in-studio interviews. I reminded them that it was only a little over forty-eight hours since the incident went down and that I was exhausted from the morning. They understood so we scheduled a phone interview for mid-afternoon and then I would appear later that evening, via phone, as part of a panel on Vinnie Politian's "Prime News" show on HLN. The other calls were from concerned friends and I returned those as well. Now it was time to relax. I planned on joining Andrea upstairs for a nap but the couch was so much closer. I'd just "rest my eyes" as my mother used to say when she'd fall asleep on the couch, for a few minutes before grabbing a few hours sleep.

After about forty-five minutes of "resting my eyes", my phone woke me up with a text message. At this time, as I do now, I had a flip phone and when a new text would come in, "NEW MESSAGE" would light up in white letters on the display. When I looked down, I saw in red letters "URGENT MESSAGE". This had never happened before. I'm not the type of person anyone ever needs to urgently get in contact with. I opened it up and honestly, one of the coolest messages I've EVER received was staring me in the face. It said "THIS IS EMAD FROM FOX 5 IN NY. PLEASE CALL ME ASAP. DANA WHITE WANTS TO MEET YOU!!"

I'd like to say that I played it off rather cool, like "I'm sure he does…why wouldn't he?" That is not exactly what happened. My reaction was something like this "Holy fuck, Dana White wants to meet me!" I admit, my enthusiasm was tempered a bit when I realized that he was probably in Las Vegas and that maybe we'd meet *eventually*. Even still, I had to call Emad back ASAP!

Chances are you've at least *heard* of Dana White. Even greater chances are that you have an opinion of Dana White. Dana is the type of guy who evokes emotion, either positive or negative, but emotion nonetheless. Dana is the boss, the man who runs the previously mentioned UFC, the Ultimate Fighting Championship, along with brothers Lorenzo and Frank Fertitta. Dana is the face of the UFC. Some people have an issue with that, some do not. I do not and never have. I have always been a fan of Dana's since the trio took over the UFC. They've brought the organization, and the sport of Mixed Martial Arts in general, to heights that nobody could have predicted when they purchased the struggling company from the Semaphore Entertainment Group in early 2001. After some early struggles, the company is now enjoying amazing success and the UFC is pretty much as mainstream as you can get. The UFC Twitter account now regularly "retweets" celebrities during their events who've probably never heard of Dan Severn, Ken Shamrock, Gary Goodridge, Oleg Taktarov or Tank Abbott. Such events pump millions into the economies of the cities they're held in. Any city would love to have a live UFC event at their local venue. What kind of foolish state would still have professional mixed martial arts banned? As of this writing, there is but one. That's right, New York!

I like Dana because he tells it like it is. It may be something you don't like or something you don't want to hear, but he gives it to you straight and you're never left wondering where you stand with him. Now I'm getting a text from someone named Emad telling me Dana White wants to meet me. *Me?*

During the course of my morning interviews, I'd mentioned my miserable attempt at the single-leg takedown. I'd also mentioned how I had no formal training and how I must have picked it up through osmosis from all the MMA I've watched and more specifically, the UFC.

I called Emad back and he told me that then-UFC public relations Master, the great Jim Byrne, contacted Fox 5 because Dana wanted to meet me. I said I was honored, but I questioned when this would take place since Dana was probably in Las Vegas. Emad told me that Dana was actually in New York and he wanted to meet me that night and asked if was interested. Again, I'd like to say that I said "well, *maybe* I can make time for Dana" but I'm pretty sure I blurted out something frantic that resembled "absolutely" and he told me he'd call me after he sorted out the details with Jim. Thankfully, they didn't keep me waiting long. I heard back from Jim and Emad and it was all set. The UFC would send a car for Andrea and I and we'd meet Dana at the Peninsula Hotel later that evening. Remember when I told I Andrea "there's no fucking way I'm coming back to the city today"? Like I said, never say never. The only catch was, this was a Fox 5 NY exclusive, and I couldn't tell anyone besides my family. Are you kidding?? I wanted to tell EVERYBODY! First, I had to tell Andrea. I asked Dominic to go upstairs and wake up mommy. You know, to tell her we were going back to city!

She came downstairs and asked me what I was talking about. I made it very clear earlier about my intentions to relax and I can be quite stubborn. When I told her about the meeting, she lost her mind! She was just as pumped as I was... well almost!

I did the first phone interview and then tried to stop watching the clock. Time seemed like it was going backwards. I wanted "tonight" to get here so I could go meet Dana. I remember the driver being delayed due to traffic (it's New York after all) and he arrived shortly before I was scheduled to appear on the Vinnie Politan show. That whole interview was done on the way to the Peninsula.

I remember pulling up to the hotel and upon entering; Jim Byrne was there to greet us. The Peninsula Hotel is amazing. Certainly a place I didn't belong in even when my head wasn't littered with staples and my left eye wasn't busted up. It's the kind of place I'd get stares just walking by it! Jim was amazing. He asked if we needed anything and he brought us to a banquet room. I met the UFC's Craig Borsari and an executive from Spike whose name escapes me now. There was a photographer there who snapped some pictures of me and then we pretty much just talked for a while until Jim told us that Dana was on his way down. I may as well have been a kid that was just alerted Santa Claus was on his way to meet him.

I recently asked Jim what he remembered about that day and he said "I know Dana was in town for meetings with TV execs…he had called me before he took off from Vegas and said "find that guy before I land". That became my mission, to find you so Dana could congratulate you for stopping a madman. He had heard you used some of the things you'd seen on UFC."

Dana came in, greeted us and was pure class. I recounted the series of events for him and he was all ears. Here's a guy that I had a million questions for and he was hanging on my every word. I kept saying "I can't believe this" because Dana's a guy I've always wanted to meet and now here he was. I was afraid I was going to "wake up" and it would have all been a dream. We had a great chat, just amazing, and Dana brought some UFC goodies as well. Some shirts, a limited edition UFC Coach bag for Andrea and a copy of the amazing UFC book "Octagon" which he signed "To Joe You Are An Amazing Human Being, Dana White". He then invited the whole family to the upcoming UFC 128 event in Newark, NJ and invited Andrea and I to watch the event at his table with him. Are. You. Kidding. Me? I am very loyal and I did give Dana some grief about one of his recent releases, my favorite fighter, Keith Jardine. Dana took it in stride and actually thought it was cool I was standing up for Keith. Dana then offered to pay for a room for Andrea and I at the Peninsula to basically get a rest from the insanity of the last seventy-two hours. I thanked him but declined because I wanted to be home with my kids. He was able to coerce us to stay for Valentine's Day dinner at the hotel on his dime. As Dana went upstairs to make the arrangements, I approached Jim again to thank him for the swag and he laughed and said "Joe, you haven't seen anything yet! ". Dana came back, escorted us to the restaurant, congratulated me again and said that someone would be in touch to handle the arrangements for the event.

Just as an aside, while Dana was talking to someone else, I turned to Andrea and said "I wonder if Chuck will be there?" Chuck is Chuck Liddell, one of the baddest dudes to ever walk the planet. Dana didn't quite hear me and he asked me to repeat it and I told him I was wondering if Chuck would be there because he was Joey and Dominic's favorite fighter. Dana said something to the effect of "if your kids want him there, he'll be there". That was awesome.

Needless to say, I stuck out like a sore thumb in the restaurant that evening. Not to sound like an absolute bumpkin, but I'd never eaten at a restaurant where the prices weren't listed on the menu. The food was insane. The service was insane and the hostess couldn't have been any nicer. Definitely the coolest Valentine's Day we've ever had.

With Founder and Chairman of GLORY Sports International, Pierre Andurand

Chapter Thirteen

As cool as Valentine's Day was, the following day was going to be the exact opposite. This was the day I'd have to testify before the Grand Jury to indict Maksim Gelman. Needless to say this was my first Grand Jury testimony so I didn't know what to expect. I was nervous but also excited. The sooner Gelman ended up behind bars for life, the better off society in general would be. I was more than happy to be a part of that.

As I was getting dressed, I had the Fox 5 morning show on in the background. While this was no longer THE story, the fact that testimony was being given today still warranted attention. I remember prior to them going to a commercial, they teased the next segment as "hear what one of Maksim Gelman's relatives had to say about him…coming up next!" Naturally I was curious. Many times, families stick together through anything and I figured this would be the case. Maybe a relative would blame somebody for his actions or just be in total denial about his attacks. I was pleasantly surprised when they reported that one of Gelman's uncles said "my nephew is an animal and deserves to be put away". Honestly, I didn't see that coming.

My sister drove Andrea & myself to the Assistant District Attorney's office to meet with him prior to testifying. We were brought to a room where we waited for a few minutes. Our lunch order was taken and A.D.A. James Lin came by to bring me to his office to brief me on what I could expect. He was basically going to ask me questions and I was going to answer them honestly and under oath. I told him my version of events regarding the confrontation. I even used action figures (his, not mine) to describe what happened. I admit, when we were recounting the incident, the thing that struck me odd was how casually he spoke of Gelman banging on the door and then the other passenger tapping on the door as well. He actually brought that up to me first. I knew he had spoken with Officers Howell and Taylor and I figured that they told him that. In my head I'm thinking "is this really ok for him (or them) that they knew it was Gelman banging on the door PLUS they acknowledge the second gentleman trying to get them to come out?" I just went with it. I was going to tell the truth so I was fine.

A.D.A. Lin also showed me some photos that were taken at the hospital. These were by far the most gruesome images of me that were taken. They were pictures of the back of my head and my face prior to any stitching or stapling. The way my head was sewn up, the scar is somewhat horizontal. In these pictures, the wound is almost completely vertical meaning that when I was sewn back together; the doctor literally had to pull the skin together. How's that for a visual? In one of the images, you can see my skull. Nobody in my family has ever seen these and I hope they never do.

He brought me back to the waiting area where Andrea and my sister were and shortly after that, our food arrived. After I finished eating, none other than Officers Howell & Taylor joined us in the waiting area. Keep in mind that at this point, while I had my doubts about their actions, or lack thereof, I still did not have concrete proof to verify it. Even still, things were awkward. Maybe they didn't like all the attention I was getting since the truth came out. Before I did any interviews, the NYPD propaganda machine had hailed both officers as heroes. Now here I come with the real story and I may have messed things up for them. I really didn't know. Fortunately for me, I was escorted by A.D.A Lin back to another room for one last meeting prior to being brought across the street to the court house. Something amazing happened during this meeting.

While he was talking, a call came in from a number I didn't recognize. It was from the 404 area code. I let it go to voicemail. When Lin left the room for a minute, I played the message and it was none other than MY hero that day, Alfred Douglas. In all my interviews, I made sure to mention the good samaritan who saved my life and how I'd love to talk to him. I didn't know his name but I figured if I mentioned him enough, maybe something good would come out of it. Before he even introduced himself in the message, I got goosebumps hearing his distinctive accent. I was so excited to hear from him, but I had other business to attend to at the moment.

A few moments later Lin returned. We made our way across the street and I was escorted in before the Grand Jury. I can't remember how many jurors there were, but it was more than I expected. It was pretty much the question and answer session I expected it to be and I did get emotional at times and had to take some deep breaths. The thing I remember most was when A.D.A Lin passed around the photos of my head. The jury was horrified. Many couldn't even look at them. I was actually watching them while I was talking. I felt bad for them. They didn't need to see that, nobody did. When the questioning was completed, Lin asked the jurors if they had any questions. I believe I needed to clarify a thing or two and then I was free to go. I was instructed to wait outside.

The waiting area was pretty well-occupied and I actually ended up sitting next to Officer Taylor. She asked me how it was and I told her what went on. I don't remember how the subject came up about me passing out, but I remember her telling me that when I passed out, they thought I died because my eyes were still open and I told her that I remember hearing one of them call me "likely". She froze; She said "you remember that?" to which I said, "of course, I remember everything from that day. I remember when you wanted to mace Gelman and your partner told you not to", she said "you remember that too?" and all I said again was "I told you I remember *everything*".

I was then instructed that I was free to go. My services were no longer required. I met Andrea and my sister and we were on our way home. My sister was not happy.

She basically had questions about what they did or didn't do that day. As stated earlier, my sister is also NYPD. She explained to me that cops will, as in any line of work, speak in "copspeak" when they're around each other. In other words, whatever line of work you the reader are in, you may speak to someone in the same field with work related jargon that the average person wouldn't understand. Andrea even added, "most of the time, I had no idea what they were talking about". My sister said that a few things bothered her. First, in relation to Officer Howell, when she would ask him questions, he would give general answers, almost avoiding specifics. She said when she questioned Officer Taylor she basically kept saying things like "you know, I really don't remember". My sister said "how can you not remember the most traumatic arrest and day in your life?'. Angela said something is definitely up with them. Her thoughts coupled with the questions I already had, further made me wonder if it is possible all of this could have been avoided?

We made our way back to my mother's house and gave her the details of the day's events. We'd have dinner then we'd pack to get ready to go home the next day. I appreciated everything everyone had done for us, but I was ready to get back to Philadelphia. I'd had my fill of New York, no doubt about that. A friend of mine, a former co-worker from MSG, Dylan Wanagiel contacted me and said a friend of his, MMA writer extraordinaire Mike Chiappetta was interested in doing a story on me and we worked it out that we'd do the interview Wednesday in the car as Andrea was driving home. As for now, it was time to eat, pack, and rest.

Chapter Fourteen

Finally on Wednesday, February 16th, we were heading back home to Philadelphia. Staying at my mother's during the first few days was not only convenient with the back and forth to and from Manhattan; it was just nice to be around my family during my darkest hour. That being said, I really wanted to get home. I wanted to be in my own neighborhood, read my local papers, watch my local channels and enjoy some Wawa decaf. Not only that, the kids had missed a full week of school and Andrea had missed a week of work. As much as I needed rest to aid in my recovery, part of my recovery also included my home life to return to as normal as possible under the circumstances.

The ride from Long Island to Northeast Philadelphia generally takes us about two and a half hours. For this ride home, most of that time was taken up by a phone interview I did with former mmafighting.com writer Mike Chiappetta. To be honest, I loved doing this interview. Sure we talked about the incident, that was a given. Most of all though, we talked MMA and if we were talking MMA, we weren't talking Gelman nonsense. It was a really fun interview. Mike's a terrific writer and an even better person. He mentioned the incident but he let me talk about being an MMA fan, about meeting Dana White and even wrangled a quote or two from Andrea. His story ran later that night and I loved it from the first read. Like I said, Mike's a great guy and I always enjoy catching up with him at UFC events whenever possible.

Thanks to Mike, before I knew it we were crossing into Pennsylvania from New Jersey. We were almost home. We just had two stops to make. First, Wawa. Man, that was one of the best decaf's I've ever had. Second, we had to stop at Modell's. The police kept my clothes as evidence and that included my sneakers. The only other pair I had were my gym sneakers. A few people in Modell's recognized me. It's not every day Frankenstein's Monster walks into a store to buy size 13 Nike's. Everyone had very nice things to say and I appreciated that.

We pulled into the driveway and we were greeted by "WELCOME HOME JOE" signs and I found out later it was our friend Kathleen and her daughter Nina. That was awesome. It was finally nice to walk inside our own place and collapse. First, I had to check the house phone voicemail. I was curious as to how many messages were waiting for us. I don't remember how many, but there were dozens. Thankfully, most had been from media outlets who also managed to find my cell phone number. One of the messages was from a writer from the Philadelphia Daily News named Will Bunch. I called him back and we agreed that we'd do the interview the following day. The paper would also send a photographer over to snap some pictures at some point. I'm almost positive the rest of the day was spent in my bed, intermittently sleeping, watching television or listening to Alice In Chains on my iPod.

Waking up in my own bed was a pleasure. While I wasn't sleeping through the night, little by little my sleep was improving. Let's be honest, it was still awful, but even the slightest improvement was cause for celebration. I knew I had some phone calls to make that day but I also knew I'd be doing a lot of that from my bed. Andrea was kind enough to make a Wawa run for me and a little while later; I called Will Bunch for the Philly Daily News interview. We had a nice chat and he ended it by telling me that he couldn't promise we'd be the cover story, but that he'd be pushing for it. The last thing the City of Philadelphia needed was my mug on the cover of "The People Paper". Andrea and the boys thought it would be cool and I knew my parents would get a kick out of it so I figured if it was to be, then why not?

Before the end of the day Thursday, Mike Chiappetta texted me and told me one of the fighters I mentioned during our interview had read his story and wanted to contact me. I was floored. To say I was excited would be an understatement. He told me they wanted to surprise me and I was ok with that....*initially.* When Mike interviewed me, I rattled off dozens of names of fighters I admire and he whittled it down to four mentions in the opening paragraph of the article. They were Joey Villasenor, Dan Severn, Eddie Alvarez and Keith Jardine, owner of one of the two best nicknames in the history of sports. Keith is "The Dean of Mean". I gave Mike permission to give my number out and then I waited...and waited.... and waited some more. It's been said "patience is a virtue". If that's the case, I was about as virtuous as a two-dollar hooker. I'm not sure if those actually exist, you just always hear them referenced though. Am I right?

Now the guessing game started. Maybe it was Villasenor because in the article, Mike wrote how I took Andrea to see an EliteXC event at the Prudential Center in Newark, NJ. That event was the first MMA event to appear on network television on CBS and it featured a man named Kimbo Slice in the main event. Kimbo was an internet street-fighting sensation who was signed by EliteXC and became one of the organizations flag-bearers. Many people went to that event to see Kimbo. I did not. Andrea did not. I went to see two fighters in particular. Nick Serra from Long Island and Joey Villasenor. Nick's fight didn't go as I had hoped and his opponent's dad was sitting across the aisle from us. I've never asked Nick what happened in that fight and I never will, but I knew something was wrong. He wasn't himself. The only saving grace was seeing the father of his opponent burst into tears when his son, Matt Makowski got his hand raised. Being a father myself, it was a truly a touching moment. Nick vs. Makowski was part of the undercard. Villasenor was on the main card.

Andrea is a huge MMA fan, but at that time, she didn't know about a lot of the fighters outside the UFC so she rooted for the guys I rooted for. Joey was fighting Phil Baroni or as he's also known, the "New York Badass". I've never been a huge fan of Phil's. He's always enjoyed playing the heel and I've never really cared for that. I don't know Phil at all and he could be a great guy but as a fighter, I generally rooted against him. That night, I was definitely in the minority. Baroni had his fans in the stands and when he came out, he received a very nice ovation. As was generally the case, he took his time getting to the cage. That always drove me nuts. Joey waited patiently in the cage. He handled it better than I did actually. I didn't think this fight would go to the ground at all since both guys like to stand and throw and they both throw HARD! Phil finally got to the cage and seventy-one seconds later, the fight was over, TKO for Joey. That was a fun night. I didn't care what happened during the rest of the card.

I didn't think it was Severn. Dan is a pioneer for the sport and one of the all-time great wrestlers. If he had called, it would have been amazing but for his sake, he's probably lucky he didn't. Dan's had over one hundred twenty five fights so we may still be on the phone! It would have been very to cool to talk old-school UFC with someone who was a huge part of it though.

I thought it could have been Eddie Alvarez. Eddie's a Philly guy so I figured he may have seen the story on the news. He also seemed like a guy who'd do that. Eddie's famous for having his wife and kids right down cage or ringside for his fights and always has kisses and hugs for them when the fights are over. He really humanizes the sport. It always kind of bothered me that Philadelphia didn't make a bigger deal of Eddie. He's always been one of the best in his weight-class and Philly has such a storied fighting history. Philadelphia embraces their own like few others, yet Eddie never seemed to get the attention I felt he'd earned and deserved.

Finally I remember saying to Andrea, "Imagine if it's Keith?" I first noticed Keith Jardine when he was a member of the second season of the Ultimate Fighter. He was very handsome with a shaved head and long goatee…just like someone else I know. In reality, I was very curious about him since it seemed like absolutely nobody in the house wanted any part of him. Thanks to the internet, I found his fight card and searched for his fight videos. The ones I couldn't find on the web were immediately ordered on dvd. Once I watched several of his fights, I was hooked. Ironically, many know Keith as a brawler because he likes to stand and throw and he's also the owner of some of the most vicious leg-kicks in the business, but in many of his early fights, he did a lot of fighting on the ground. Keith didn't win TUF 2, but he did fight on the Finale and he dismantled Kerry Schall with the leg kicks I mentioned. That was awesome. I started really following his career from that point. UFC fighters generally get more press than any other fighters in MMA and the more I read up on him, the more I liked him. He was just a blue-collar guy who liked to fight and was good at it. He was confident but never cocky and yes, there is a difference. To this day my two favorite fights are his wins over perennial fan-favorite Forrest Griffin and the legend Chuck Liddell. For as long as I watch MMA, I doubt anything will top those two.

I started freaking out thinking that Keith might call me. What would I say? I had so many questions and so much to talk about. What do you say when one of your heroes calls to talk to you? I'm pretty sure I was driving Andrea crazy. Andrea had to go to the store (and also to Wawa for a decaf for me) but she was hanging around to see who was going to call.

I texted Mike and asked him to reveal who it was. I couldn't take it anymore. I was going nuts. How silly I must have looked, a forty year old man acting like a child. I had to know though. He relented and revealed that it was indeed Keith Jardine. He told me to make sure to pick up the phone when I see a 505 area code.

Finally, just as Andrea was walking out the door, the phone rang. It was indeed a call from "the 505". I know I yelled "it's Keith, it's Keith" and she came back in. I took a deep breath, composed myself and very coolly and casually answered the phone. "Hello" I said and the voice on the other end said "Hey Joe, this is Keith Jardine. How's it goin' buddy?"

Chapter Fifteen

"How's it going?" The Dean of Mean just asked me how it's going. What a thrill. I've said it before and I'll say it again, I admire those who do things that the average person can't do. Here's a man I've admired for so long and he heard that I mentioned him in an article and he thought to call me. This is a man who makes his living in a combat sport. Only a small percentage of people in the world can say that. *He* wants to know how *I'm* doing? Forget me; I have so much to say to him!

Keith heard about my story when the aforementioned Joey Villasenor alerted him to the Mike Chiappetta article. Knowing Keith as I do now, I'm not surprised at all he reached out. He asked about my story and I gave him all the details... but I really wanted to talk to him about his fights. When I brought up the Forrest Griffin fight, I think his answer was something like "thanks man, but how are you feeling?" When I brought up the Liddell fight, I received a similar response. Finally when I told him that it pisses me off that he got robbed in the Stephan Bonnar fight (a fight he CLEARLY won 29-28), he did laugh a little but quickly changed the focus back to me.

At some point Keith mentioned that he had a fight coming up in a few weeks in Albuquerque and asked if I was aware. Although I was disappointed it was a smaller show and wouldn't be televised, I was very aware. He asked if I'd be interested in seeing it live and I said of course I would, but finances would prevent me from making the trip. He told me that he had spoken to the promoter, Lenny Fresquez, and that Andrea and I would be their guests. The flights, hotel, tickets, everything would be paid for. I honestly started to cry. I was so touched. I didn't know how to react and tears of joy were the first thing that happened. I think I thanked him a million times. We spoke for a little while longer when he relented and let me talk about some of his fights and then he said Coach Wink would be in touch the next day to get the details. Coach Wink? Cool!

I texted Mike to let him know the call had been made and to thank him for probably the hundredth time. He was very happy for me. I was grateful because his article was the conduit to the connection. I will always be in Mike's debt for writing that piece.

I think at some point, I collapsed into a moderately deep sleep and woke up early the next day before anyone else. The whole family had been through so much this past week so I crept around the house trying not to wake anybody up. I was hoping they'd all sleep until noon. I wanted to get out and get some fresh air. It was morning, so of course my Wawa decaf was calling me. I put my sneakers on and made my way out. Just before I reached to close the door behind me, a gigantic light bulb crashed onto my head….CHECK THE INTERNET; YOU MAY BE ON THE COVER OF THE PHILLY DAILY NEWS! I made my way back to the home computer, went to the website and damn, there it was…my face on the front cover with the headline; CUTS AND GUTS. I will admit, the headline is pretty cool. The face, well, what can I say? Sorry about that.

When I went to Wawa, all the workers were excited. Remember, I stopped there every day so these people were like good friends. We always chatted it up about sports, especially baseball. Being a rabid Braves fan in Philadelphia during the Phillies run of dominance wasn't always easy, but that group always made the debates fun. I hadn't seen any of them in almost a week but they probably heard about the story and obviously saw the paper they were selling that day. It was somewhat comical to see people look down at their paper, look up at me and look down at their paper again. I was probably there for about thirty minutes talking to people. Everybody was so amazing. When I got home, I think everybody was awake. I showed them the paper. Andrea loved it and Joey and Dom were pumped. I loved seeing their faces. Andrea asked me how many copies I bought and I told her one. She said "One! You bought ONE copy?" and I said "yes, how many do I normally buy every day?" She answered "how many days are you on the COVER?" She had me there. She immediately went out and bought several copies that we could give to friends and family.

Later that day I received a call from Dana White's then-assistant, a great woman named Chari Cuthbert. She asked for the clothes sizes for myself, Andrea and the boys and wanted to confirm that Chuck Liddell was indeed the boy's favorite fighter. I supplied her with that info and she told me to contact her if I ever needed anything else or if I had any questions. Other than that, I caught up with some friends on the phone, watched some television and made an appointment to see my doctor. That weekend was spent doing a whole lot of nothing.

On Monday I had an appointment with my doctor, Dr. Allan Wohl. Dr. Wohl was born to be a doctor. He is a true gentleman and he treats each patient like we are his only patient. Most doctors could take a lesson from him. Over our ten year doctor and patient relationship, I considered him a friend and I think he felt the same way about me, about our whole family actually. We talked in the lobby for a few minutes and then we went to an examination room. As he went over my hospital records, he was furious that Bellevue did not test me for Hepatitis, did not test me for HIV and most of all, that they actually discharged me so soon after the incident. He took blood, did all the testing and was happy to report that I was free from all viruses. I did all my follow-up appointments with Dr. Wohl. He removed the staples, removed the stitches and became my default therapist, always lending an ear for me to vent or voice concerns about my recovery and my future in general. I will be forever grateful to Dr. Wohl for his friendship and his care.

Upon arriving home, there were several boxes in our driveway, probably seven or eight in all. We had no idea where they were from. I got out of the car and saw the shipping label on all of them. They were from Zuffa LLC, the parent company of the UFC. The UFC had sent us boxes upon boxes of merchandise costing several thousands of dollars. Talk about Christmas in February! It probably took the four of us two hours to go through everything. It was absolutely incredible.

With the "Dean of Mean"
Keith Jardine

Chapter Sixteen

After our "UFC Christmas in February" festivities were over, I made my way to the computer to send a thank you e-mail to Dana White & Cheri. I had an e-mail from UFC Vice President Reed Harris waiting for me. Reed was making contact as he was going to be the person who took care of us at UFC 128. I thought it was pretty cool as I knew of Reed from his days of running the WEC. I'm proud to call Reed and his wife Laura friends. They are amazing people. After a brief e-mail exchange, he told me he'd be in touch as the event got closer.

On February 24th, the Islanders would be in town to play the Flyers. The game had extra special meaning to us as the Flyers reached out to our family and wanted to honor us. They would announce me on the Jumbrotron and none other than Flyers legend Bob "The Hound" Kelly would present me with a Flyers jersey. A few days earlier, I was on the same arena floor as an Honorary Ringmaster for the Ringling Brothers and Barnum and Bailey Circus. That was insane. Now I'm back in the stands and I'm getting a standing ovation from 19,000 people. I cannot tell you what that feels like. It was electric! I know I teared up. After the game, we went down by the Islanders dressing room and I was waiting for a few of the guys to come out and head coach Jack Capuano told me to come in the room to see all the guys. I already had a relationship with several of the players and coaches, including assistant coach Dean Chynoweth who joked, "this is embarrassing, you're an Islanders guy, we have to do something for you and I can't believe the

Flyers did it first". Deano's always been great to me as I've known him since his American Hockey League days when he was a teammate of Dean Ewen's. I was allowed to address the team and I basically told them that one of the proudest moments I have ever had as an Islanders fan was the aforementioned "revenge" game against Pittsburgh. I told them they were truly a team and they should look at the guy in the stall next to them with pride because they knew they'd have your back. Zenon Konopka said "I knew you'd like that one buddy! ". I chatted with the boys for a few more minutes and then we made our way over to the Flyers locker room.

I met a bunch of the Flyers players and staff. Whether you're a Flyers fan or not, one thing you must know is that the organization is 1st class. From top to bottom, they treat everyone with respect. It was great to meet some of the guys, including Mike Richards whose number "18" I requested to be stitched on the jersey when I was asked what number I wanted. I was also able to reconnect with Chris Pryor who was also a teammate of both Dean's during his time in the Islanders organization. I met longtime Flyers PR guru Zack Hill and we had a great chat about "old-time Flyers hockey". All in all, it was truly a memorable evening.

The following week meant back to work. Lincoln Center told me to take all the time I needed to recover and to come back when I was ready. I'm honestly not sure I was ready to go back to work, but I was definitely ready to get back into a routine. One of the people I was looking forward to seeing was my boss, Pete Meyers. Pete's a great guy and even though his sisters are going to mock me for putting that in print, it's true. This is the kind of guy Pete is, my first few days back at work, Pete would meet me at Penn Station to ride the subway with me to work. I thought that was awesome. I think it was more for support than protection and I really appreciated it. After a few days though, I told him I was ok to go it alone. I'd have to do it eventually so let's get back on the horse as soon as possible. I did have some apprehension and anxiety but I made myself go to the first car and sit in the same exact seat as much as possible. Whether it helped or not, I don't know, but the point was that I could do it.

A few days later, Andrea and I were boarding a plane to Albuquerque, New Mexico to see Keith Jardine fight in the main event of the "Double Threat" MMA show. When we landed, we were immediately taken to the Route 66 Hotel and Casino for the press conference and weigh-ins. We walked in just as it was about to begin. I met Mr. Fresquez and he introduced me to Keith. We said a quick hello and then settled in for the press conference. Once the weigh-ins were over, I met several members of Team Jackson-Winkeljohn, including Michael Johnson, Julie Kedzie, Brendan Weafer, John Dodson and Travis Marx. It was great to meet them all and I'm still in touch with some of them to this day.

When things settled down, we went up to Keith's room as he was going through the rehydration process and we met his fiancé and fellow fighter Jodie Esquibel, Keith's manager John Madrid and one of the most unique people I've ever met, Tait Fletcher. We chatted for a bit and then Andrea and I went for lunch. Ironically after we were done eating, we had a nice conversation with Keith's opponent for the following night, Aron Lofton, and his family who were in town for the fight.

Fight day arrived and after breakfast, Andrea & I wandered into the arena to check things out. When we got there, Keith was warming up in the cage. When he was done, we went to the sound booth and he asked me for suggestions for his walk-out music. Predictably, I suggested "Angry Chair" by Alice In Chains. That's what I'd walk out to if I possessed either the talent or the balls to fight for a living. He politely declined and went with a song he'd used before, "Bog" by the Wicked Tinkers. After that, he went to rest and Andrea and I played the slots. We won enough to cover all the shirts we bought for everybody so I'd call it a rousing success.

Hours later, Andrea & I were in the VIP section with some of Mr. Fresquez's friends and family and many members of Team Jackson/Winkeljohn. We met a few more members of the team, including Coach Jackson and Coach Winkeljohn, Isaac Vallie-Flagg and UFC great and future Hall of Famer "Suga" Rashad Evans. It's amazing to watch fights surrounded by people who do it for a living. They see things the average fan doesn't see and it was an amazing learning experience.

Some of the matches ended earlier than expected and some time needed to be filled so Mr. Fresquez approached me and asked "how do you feel about getting in the cage with Rashad?" and I said "ummm, I don't have to fight him, do I?". We entered the cage to a HUGE ovation. I guess entering the cage with one the guys on whom the foundation of one the greatest combat sports teams was built will have that effect on people. We both spoke briefly and after a very short version of my story, the Albuquerque faithful showed me some love as well.

Eventually it was time for the main event. Aron Lofton entered the cage and once the Wicked Tinkers bagpipes started blaring, it was time for "The Dean of Mean" to make his entrance. The crowd went bonkers, including the VIP section. The two exchange some lethal blows and Lofton caught Keith with a nice shot but Keith quickly recovered and almost as if a switch was flipped, went on the offensive and scored the TKO victory at 3:30 of the first round. It was definitely one of the greatest nights of my life and being included in it by Keith himself means more to me than he'll ever know.

After the post-fight press conference Andrea and I joined Jodie and Dave Jardine, Keith's father in the dressing room. When Keith came out and was embraced by his dad, that was awesome to see. You can tell how much they mean to each other. I was introduced to Dave shortly thereafter and checked to see if my hand was still attached. The man has some grip and huge paws! Dave is such a gentle man, but I bet if the shit hit the fan, he'd take care of business without much problem.

We went back to Keith's room for a very unhealthy late dinner and then headed to the bar for a few beers with some of the team. A little while later, we went back to the room to pack for our flight out on Saturday. The next morning was VERY eventful as somebody who shall remain nameless, but whom I was rooming with…and lives with me…and has two children with me realized she'd lost the camera. We almost didn't go to the airport. She was beside herself. We eventually made our flight but the fact we didn't have our camera ruined it for the person who shall remain nameless.

Thankfully, a few days later, a very nice woman named Yvette Gonzales posted some of the pictures on Facebook to Keith's attention and Andrea saw them. Yvette found the camera in the bar after we left and took it home. We made contact and Yvette was nice enough to send the camera back to us. Talk about saving the day!

Back home to Philadelphia meant back to work. Pete didn't overload me with work and I really should thank all my co-workers for picking up the slack both in my absence and even after I came back. I wasn't ready to do my fair share of the work. Then one night as I was leaving work and on the phone with a friend, I noticed something. I was being followed.

With "Suga" Rashad Evans

Chapter Seventeen

If you're familiar at all with Lincoln Center, you know there is a giant fountain on the plaza centrally located between the Metropolitan Opera House, Avery Fisher Hall and the David Koch Theater. This particular evening, I was on the phone with my buddy Brent from Texas just bringing him up to speed on all that had gone on. He had seen it on the news, but this was my first opportunity to speak to him myself. Knowing I had some time until my train, I circled the fountain a few times while chatting it up with Brent. Even before this incident, I always tried to be aware of my surroundings and have always made use of my peripheral vision. Not ten feet behind me, a man is following me step for step. I told Brent I'd call him back. I needed to find out who this guy was.

I slowed my pace ever so slightly but my "shadow" did not and in a matter of seconds he was close. I turned around quickly and said "can I help you?" in such a manner as to startle the man. My approach worked as he immediately attempted to settle me down by explaining that he wasn't looking for trouble. He just needed to speak with me. He asked me if I was "*the* Joe Lozito" from the subway incident which was probably rhetorical at this point since I still sported the wounds. He told me that he was one of the members of the Grand Jury that I testified in front of to indict Gelman. Being the cynic that I am, I asked him to prove it. The newspapers published where I worked and anybody could conceivably come to my job and claim to be a Grand Juror. Then it hit me, if he could describe the photos I was shown by A.D.A. Linn, then he was most definitely telling the truth. He described each one in graphic detail. He now had my trust.

He proceeded to tell me that Gelman was being indicted no matter what the police had to say. He told me how powerful my testimony was and described the scene in the room after I exited as being somewhat surreal. He told me how much of an impact I had made not only on himself, but on many of the other jurors. He told me that when he went home, he "googled" me and read several articles and watched some of the news interviews I had done. He said that I needed to stop giving so much credit to the police. I said "listen, I know the police have a tough job and my sister is a cop. I respect what they do" and he stopped me cold and said "forget about how you feel about the police in *general.....these two cops* hung you and everybody else on that train out to dry that day!". Startled, I asked him to elaborate.

Anticipating his reply, my heart started racing. As I mentioned several times previously, I had already had my doubts as to what happened behind me that day but nothing could prepare me for what I was about to hear. He said "Officer Howell testified that when Gelman was looking down at you and when you were looking up at him before the fight had started, Howell actually opened the door to come out, but when Gelman reached in his jacket, Howell thought he had a gun.....so he closed the door and stayed inside with his partner".

Just let that sink in for a minute. Here you have an officer who took an oath to "serve and protect" admitting that the man he was on the train to apprehend, a man who at this point was a wanted, spree-killing fugitive...excuse me, a wanted, spree-killing, *police-impersonating* fugitive, a man with a well-documented history of violence who was now mere inches away from the officer. Yet this veteran officer, armed with a loaded gun, a police baton, mace and the element of surprise, this officer with double-digit years of experience, this officer who the NYPD hailed as a hero, took cover in the locked motormen's cab with his partner and left a subway car full of unarmed civilians to deal with a murderer. Hung us out to dry indeed!

I was stunned. I didn't know what to say. It literally was like being attacked all over again, only this time, by the *alleged* "good guys". The only positive is that now all my doubts could be pieced together and everything made sense. When the officers were faced with mortal danger, even with all the advantages they owned, they took the coward's way out. I took a few moments to let it sink in. I had to maintain my composure since I had my 2 ½ commute home to Philadelphia ahead and I couldn't tell Andrea this news on the phone. This was a face to face discussion. I thanked the man for helping me out with that information and we went our separate ways. This was the longest ride home I've ever had.

Over the course of the years commuting via New Jersey Transit, I had made quite a few friends with several of the conductors. This particular ride home was no different as I can't remember who it was, but it was a conductor I was friendly with. I started telling him what I had just learned when the passenger seated in front of me apologized for listening to my story. He told me he was a lawyer and he wondering if I was going to pursue legal action. I told him absolutely. He said his name was Joseph Lemkin and he worked for a large firm but not one that could help me in this situation. He wanted to ask a colleague if he could recommend anyone for me so he gave me his card and told me to call him tomorrow. When I called, he gave me the name of a lawyer whom they thought would be perfect for me, a Long Island based attorney named Ed Chakmakian.

When I arrived home that evening, the boys were already asleep and I told Andrea that we needed to talk. I relayed the story to her and she was very upset. The same scenario repeated itself as I discussed it with my parents and my siblings and as Andrea did the same with her side of the family. It was a very difficult time for all of us as we had to accept that this entire incident could have been avoided had the police on the train just done their job!

I was off from work the next day so I did my research on Ed. I liked what I read. He seemed to be a no-nonsense, pit-bull type of lawyer and that's just what I was looking for. I'll always remember a case when I was on jury-duty and the lawyer was so timid that his client never stood a chance. I believe he was a public defender and he was awful. Based on the facts, a good, confident lawyer would have definitely made a difference in that case. I called Ed, we spoke for a few minutes and we agreed I'd make the trip up to Long Island the following week for a consultation.

After a few minutes with Ed, I liked him. He had a confidence about him that may borderline on arrogance and I say that as an absolute compliment. We had a great meeting. I told him the whole story and he was absolutely blown away. He did tell me right from the beginning that we had a tough road ahead of us. I was stunned by this and asked him to explain. He basically said that the defense Corporation Counsel was going to use was that a "special relationship" was never developed between myself and the officers and because of that, according to the law, Corporation Counsel would argue that they had no duty to protect me or anyone else on the train. I know I laughed because he had to be joking but unfortunately, the joke would turn out to be on me. He showed me several cases where they used that defense and were successful. None of them were similar to my case, but nonetheless he predicted that would be their strategy. He promised that we'd fight it full-speed ahead, but wanted to warn me about what we'd be up against.

I asked him how this process would work and he informed me that we'd file a "Notice of Claim" with our intention to bring an action against the city. We'd file our complaint and then we'd go through the "discovery" phase where we'd exchange information. After that, he warned me to not be surprised if they submitted a "motion to dismiss" which we would then be able to answer. This was a lot of information for me to handle in one meeting so we agreed that we'd do a press release, hold a press conference and take it from there. He'd be in touch when the wheels were in motion.

Since most of my family and Andrea's family still live in New York, I had the opportunity to see almost everybody shortly after the incident. I wasn't able to see my father or stepmother Dorothy since they live in Kansas but my dad flew into to Philadelphia for a visit and it was great to see him. It was very emotional and I hated that he had to see me in such bad condition. I had sent him pictures but it's always different when it's seen in person. My father, a United States Marine Vietnam Veteran and Purple-Heart recipient, presented me with the Humanitarian Service Medal which is awarded to individuals for "Meritorious participation in a significant military act or operation of a humanitarian nature, or have rendered a special service to mankind". Coming from my father it meant the world to me. He stayed with us for a few days and accompanied me when I did a spot on the "SiriusXM Fight Club" satellite radio program. The visit was a short one, but I was glad to spend time with him and show him that I was ok.

With UFC President Dana White

CHAPTER EIGHTEEN

I received a pretty cool phone call from Reed Harris that went something like this "Hey Joe, any interest in marching in the St. Patty's Day parade with Chuck?" Hmmmm, let me think about this, I have the opportunity to be a part of something historic and tag along with a UFC legend? I believe I said "Hell yeah Reed! Just tell me what to do!"

Two days later, I met Reed, Chuck, his then-fiancé, now wife Heidi and their family at the same hotel where I met Dana White a month earlier. We were driven to a specific location where we waited…and waited….and waited. There was way more waiting than marching that day. One thing I can attest to is just how accommodating Chuck Liddell was to EVERY SINGLE person who approached him. EVERYBODY wanted a picture and EVERYBODY wanted an autograph and he made time for everyone. I think Heidi had a lot to do with that as she handled everything else while Chuck met with his fans. I would guess it wasn't the first time for a situation like this.

Finally, it was time to start marching…or so we thought. Just as we were about to turn the corner, one of the higher-ups from the parade would not allow Chuck to march with his green mohawk. One of the firemen had an Irish-style hat that Chuck ended up wearing and all went well. Before I left, I met with Reed who gave me all the information I needed for the following day. That would be Friday, March 18th, the day of the UFC 128 weigh-ins. One of the most surreal weekends of my life was about to begin less than twenty-four hours from that point.

Friday morning we piled into the truck and made our way to the Hilton Newark Penn Station which was the hotel that the UFC was generous enough to put us up in for the weekend. Coincidentally it was the same hotel where most of the staff and the fighters were staying. I texted Reed when we arrived and he said he'd be there shortly. I turn around and who's there but none other than MMA legend Mark "The Hammer" Coleman. I'd love to show you the picture, but our camera crapped out. Man was I upset. Here's a guy who is a big reason I starting following the sport and now…nothing. No picture. This certainly couldn't happen again so Andrea went to a store and bought a new camera. Of course we never saw Coleman again.

Several fighters and trainers made their way through the lobby and I was happy to see Long Island's own Ray Longo. I had met Ray on the set of Ariel Helwani's show when Ray was on with UFC newcomer at the time Chris Weidman and Chris' partner in crime, fellow badass Gian Villante. I chatted with Ray for a bit in the lobby and then his fighter for the next night, Costas Philippou showed up with Pete "Drago" Sell. Costas was one of the fighters I was really looking forward to seeing battle as he was based out of Long Island with Team Serra-Longo. He took the fight on short notice and it was catch-weight bout at 195 pounds. Costas lost a decision but I was really impressed. He's a serious contender at middleweight in the UFC and now trains at Bellmore Kickboxing Academy. More on BKA later.

Before Reed showed up I was able to meet Jim Miller, Eddie Wineland and Kenny Florian. All three were very cordial and amazing to talk to. I also met UFC "jack-of-all-trades" Shanda Maloney who was amazing to us and continues to be to this day. I'm very grateful to call her a friend. When Reed showed up, we chatted for a bit and then it was off to the arena for the UFC 128 weigh-ins.

Witnessing the weigh-ins from backstage was very interesting. You really get an idea of which guys had easier weight-cuts and which guys struggled. For the big boys like Mirko Cro Cop and Brendan Schaub, they were pretty mellow as being heavyweights, I'm not sure how much, if any, weight they had to cut. There was one fighter in a lighter weight class who was basically walking around like a zombie. The weight-cut must have been brutal and coincidentally, he lost the following night. Once the weigh-ins were over, we headed to Madison Square Garden to catch the Montreal Canadiens play the New York Rangers. Unfortunately, the Rangers won, but ex-Islander James Wisniewski scored and I had a chance to chat with him for a bit after the game. We met during his short stay on the Island and he was always very classy.

The following day was UFC 128. As always, the UFC had a lot going on outside the arena and we made our way over mid-afternoon. Fighters like Chuck Liddell, Stephan Bonnar and fellow Long Islander Matt "The Terror" Serra were making appearances at various booths. Matt's long-time striking coach Ray Longo let Matt know I'd be stopping by and I can honestly tell you, Matt treated me, actually my whole family-including my brother who had joined us at this point, like we were lifelong friends. If you're an MMA fan you either love Matt Serra or think he's obnoxious. I'm here to tell you that Matt is one of the most genuine people I've ever met. Upon moving back to Long Island, I contacted Matt to let him know I wanted to enroll Joey in his kids Brazilian Jiu-Jitsu program and he told me to make sure I came by when he was there so he could speak to Joey personally. Joey watched for a bit and then we went to the back and Matt had a heart to heart talk with him and after that, Joey was sold. A few months later, Dominic signed up too. They absolutely LOVE training at Matt's Levittown Academy and I would recommend it to anyone thinking of training BJJ in the area.

Every time I'd see Matt he'd always say the same thing "when are you coming in to train buddy?" I always wanted to train, but my work schedule prevents me from following any sort of class schedule. Well, this one week, I was able to make three classes and I wanted to dive right in. My first class, I was working on forward and backward rolls. If you've seen me, you know I'm not small and yes, I'm as agile as I look...exactly. On one of the rolls, I suffered a deep bruise of the chest wall. It hurt to even breathe. Because of that, I wasn't able to attend the other two classes that week and as you're reading this, it's questionable if I've returned. I do plan on following up at some point, even if it's private lessons. I just have no idea when.

The last thing I'll say about Matt is that he's a great friend and over three years later, he's still there for me just as he was when the incident first happened. It's a tragedy he didn't get to fight at Madison Square Garden before he retired. Long Island is becoming a breeding ground for badass fighters and many owe a debt to Matt for paving the way.

As I have always done, I MUST get to the arena for the prelims. I don't get fans who only show up for the main card. Unless you have work or family commitments, I just don't understand not going for all the fights. We arrived early to grab dinner in the press-room with Reed & Laura. The UFC goes all-out and put out a nice spread. During dinner, Andrea was looking around and suddenly said "hey, it's Herb Dean!!" in reference to the veteran referee who's one of the best in the business. She said it a little louder than she probably intended and he raised his head from his plate. He was gracious enough to talk for a bit and take pictures. Every event we watch is not complete now until one of us says "hey, it's Herb Dean!!" after he's announced and gives his salute.

Walking out to the arena floor was surreal. Understand that for most events prior to this, Andrea & I would pretty much takes the escalators to the top level of the arena. Now we were on the floor, being escorted by a UFC Vice President to Dana White's table to watch an event. I really have to acknowledge how nice Laura Harris was in that she was basically Joey & Dom's babysitter that evening. Andrea and I sat cageside at Dana's table the entire night and Laura sat with Joey & Dom a row or two back for as long as they could stay awake. That was very nice of her to do that. They actually lasted for most of the event, but once they were ready for bed, my mother-in-law Doreen came to the arena to take them back to the hotel.

To be about a foot away from the UFC Octagon was amazing. Even at this point with nobody in it, it was just ridiculous to be that close. Reed would come and go while the prelims were going on as his many duties during a show have him running all over. As fans, we watch the events on television and never think twice about all the work that goes into making it flawless. I saw firsthand just how hard people like Reed, Shanda and Dave Sholler work during events. Those are just three names of many but they are the unsung heroes during these events.

One of the funnier parts of the evening was when Reed told me that "Inside MMA" wanted to interview me. "Inside MMA" is THE MMA show and it's hosted by Kenny Rice and the LEGEND, Bas Rutten. I only say it's funny because I still don't get why people wanted to talk to me and now I was going to be interviewed by Ron Kruck, a man who I'd seen interview a "who's who" in MMA and now he wants to interview me? What an honor.

At some point during the event, Dana came out along with Lorenzo & Frank Fertitta Jr. Talk about a presence; the three of them definitely have it. I again profusely thanked Dana for the experience and I now had a chance to thank the Fertitta's as well. One of the things I noticed was that Dana had a flip phone which made me happy since I sported one as well. If one of the most powerful men in sports has a flip phone, then it was good enough for me. He asked what I thought of the seats and I said "the last time we were here for a UFC event, it was UFC 111 and we sat waaaay up there" as I pointed to the top of the arena. We sat three rows from the top for that one. He smiled, put his arm around me and said "those days are over brother". I think I almost pissed myself when he said that.

There were rumors of a UFC return to Philadelphia and I asked him if it were true and he told me it was but nothing was announced yet. I asked if it would be possible to attend and Andrea punched me and said "I can't believe you're asking him that" and Dana said I could ask him for anything. He said "what's your number?" and he punched the digits into his phone and called. As the call went through, he said, "now you have my number and whenever you want tickets, just text or call me and let me know". I have to admit, that was awesome!

At one point I turned around and saw that Chuck Liddell and UFC lightweight champion Frankie Edgar were sitting behind me and I said, "holy shit, what's wrong with *this* picture? I should NEVER be sitting in front of guys like you" and Frankie laughed and patted me on the back and told me I earned it.

The fights were amazing and we still had the main event where the light-heavyweight champion Mauricio "Shogun" Rua would defend his belt against Jon "Bones" Jones. The place was electric. "Shogun" is an MMA legend and "Bones" was the new kid who was just destroying people and most felt it was a matter of when, not if, Jones would be champion. The fight was a testament as to just how tough Rua is as Jones dominated him and won in the third round. Rua took a beating and a lesser man would not have lasted as long as he did.

As Andrea and I were watching the celebration in the cage, I felt a hand on my shoulder and a voice in my ear say "man, you're EVERYWHERE aren't you?" and when I looked, it was my friend from the cage in Albuquerque, Rashad Evans who was about to enter the cage and begin the hype for the inevitable bout between he and Jones. That was awesome and I'm getting goosebumps right now typing it.

When the fights were over, we went in the back to watch the post-fight press conference. Before it started, Coach Jackson brought us into Jon Jones dressing room and it was packed with people. It was cool to be a foot away while Jon was being interviewed by Jon Anik for ESPN but even cooler to see how close Jones is with his family. It was very special to see that up close.

At some point, I did an interview with a man named "Showdown" Joe Ferraro for SportsNet up in Canada. Joe was awesome and we chatted about my incident, MMA and some hockey. Joe is truly one of the best MMA personalities out there and is passionate about his craft. I'm glad he wanted to talk to me and I'm glad we're friends to this day. He's pretty cool…for a Leafs fan!

As we headed back to the hotel, I couldn't believe it was around three AM. I did one more interview with Darcy McBride for RadioTKO in Vancouver and that was that. Back to our room for a few hours of sleep before heading out in the morning. I'm probably leaving out a ton of details but I can honestly say that the UFC 128 weekend was one of the most amazing experiences of my life.

The Lozito family at the UFC 128 weigh-ins in Newark, NJ. Photo courtesy of Chris Doucette Toronto Sun/QMI Agency

Photo credit Chris Doucette/Toronto Sun

Chapter Nineteen

Healing after something as traumatic as this incident is a slow process. Although it may be faster than a tortoise or the wheels of justice, it's painfully slow. Let's face it, I handled myself in the fight, but I got busted up pretty good. If you looked at me and you looked at Gelman after the fight, you'd see who suffered more damage. Of course the odds weren't in my favor, but nonetheless, my physical healing was, and still is, a long road. The staples come out, the stitches come out, but the scars still remain. As much as I want to put this behind me, can it ever truly be? I look in the mirror every day. The scar under my left eye is there staring back at me. When I shave my head, I need to shave over my scars. When I make a fist with my right hand, the scar at my knuckle yawns back at me. When I do *anything* with my left hand, my left thumb is quick to remind me "not so fast buddy, things are not as they once were". I think I have a very strong will but sometimes when I say I'm putting it past me, I think the person I'm trying to convince the most is myself.

The psychological scars are much more devastating to deal with. You can try to manipulate things in your mind, but ultimately, you can't fool yourself. My reality is that a guy tried to kill me. A guy brandished an eight-inch knife and literally tried to lobotomize me. The scary part is being in an enclosed environment. There's only so much room to move. So many thoughts run through your head, *if he kills me, what about my family? What happens to Andrea and my God, how does this change the lives of Joey and Dominic? Are they ruined forever?* In the moment, it's like *if he kills me, how many others will he kill? How can I stop this guy?* I don't take what Maksim Gelman did to me personally. After all, he doesn't know me. We didn't have a grudge with each other. There isn't a prior history. I was just a piece of meat to him or as Maksim called me on a documentary, a "nosey, bald guy". Maksim was on a mission that day, he was a killing machine and I was just another "object of his affection".

My psychological issues stem from why the incident had to happen at all? Why did Officer Terrance Howell and Officer Tamara Taylor take the coward's way out? Why did they hide? Were they afraid of Maksim Gelman? Did all the training in the academy coupled with all the "on the job" training since then not prepare them to deal with a man such as Gelman? Did their police issued firearms not give them any more courage? What about the police issued batons? The mace? The combination of all three PLUS the element of surprise? You mean to tell me with all this going for them, Officer Howell and Officer Taylor couldn't muster the intestinal fortitude to DO THEIR JOB that day? This is what I deal with psychologically…the "why"…or should I say the "why not".

I have had several people tell me to play the "race card". Both officers are African-American and both Maksim and I are Caucasian. I have never thought about doing that because I don't feel that race played any role in this. I feel that had I brought that up at any time, I would lose credibility and at the end of the day, my word is all I have. Bottom line is, I don't look at Officers Howell and Taylor as African-American, the only color I see when I see them is YELLOW!

Fortunately, where New York City has failed me, others were happy to prop me up and support me. Besides all that I've mentioned so far, the New York Islanders in partnership with TD Bank honored me as a "Hometown Hero" award recipient during a game against the hated Rangers. The award is given to "honor locals who go above and beyond to display exemplary courage". To be honored by an organization that I have followed since I was a little kid was truly incredible. I feel like I grew up at the Nassau Coliseum. I've had many memorable moments there; the most important was meeting my wife Andrea at an Islanders game. The night was great, not only because of the award, but because the Islanders dominated the Rangers. The game was very physical which is the way I like and the way the game should be played but the best part, no doubt, was being acknowledged on the scoreboard with Joey and Dominic by my side.

For the record, I didn't expect anyone to do anything for me. The two teams that didn't that I was really hoping would were the Philadelphia Phillies and the New York Yankees. Both organizations were aware of the incident. Before you think I'm not grateful for all that happened, my reasons for those two teams are very simple. Joey is a Phillies fan and Andrea and Dominic are Yankees fans. All that had happened so far was, for the most part, for me. Anything that was done by either ballclub would have allowed me to share the moment with the people who meant the most to me, my family. I couldn't imagine the look on Joey's face if the Phillies had done something or watching young Dom go nuts if the Yankees had done anything. Neither team is my favorite and when I say I bear no ill-will towards them, I mean it. I just wish I could have seen the boy's faces had something happened.

The one baseball team who did do something, a team who I *am* a fan of, is the Somerset Patriots of the independent Atlantic League. We have been to a ton of Patriots games. The games are always fun and in today's day and age, the Patriots provide a tremendous value for any family. We've had a great relationship with several members of the Patriots staff for years, especially Vice President Bryan Iwicki and his wife Annie. To put it simply, Bryan, and the entire staff from top to bottom "get it". It is just a tremendous organization and I can't say enough about them.

Bryan called me and asked if we were coming to Opening Night and I said we were planning to. He said "good, how do feel about throwing out a first pitch?" I was pumped. Minor league teams usually have numerous people throw out first pitches every game, it's all part of the "fan experience". Didn't matter to me if I was alone or one of a hundred, the fact that he thought of me was very humbling.

On May 6th, 2011, I took the field at TD Bank Ballpark and was told to make sure I was last in line and to wait before throwing the pitch because the public-address announcer was going to say a few things first. While I was waiting I was hanging out with two of my buddies on the team, Travis Anderson and Casey Cahill. Those two guys were awesome to my entire family from the day we met. Travis and I hit it off right away since he's a rabid MMA fan and Casey showed Joey some pitching tricks during an on-field clinic once and since then, we'd always shoot the shit when I'd get to a game. Finally, it was time to line-up.

I don't remember how many people went before me, but honestly, the only one I paid attention to was the kid in front of me. I felt enough pressure, not to throw a strike, but to just reach the plate! If this kid nailed it, the pressure would rise in a hurry. Damn if that kid didn't throw a seed! Now it was my turn. I waited until the announcer said his brief speech about what I did, took a deep breath and released. I don't remember if it was a ball or a strike, but I remember I did indeed reach the plate and whomever the catcher was (sorry, I'm embarrassed I don't remember) had a grip like a vice when he shook my hand! When I looked over at my family, there were smiles all around which was all I could hope for. Once again, the Lozito family left a Somerset Patriots game after another enjoyable time.

The Lozito men take in a Somerset Patriots game.

Chapter Twenty

Picture this, there's a madman on the loose in the city. He's attacking both specific and random people. This man holds no regard for human life and anyone that gets in his way may meet their untimely demise. The authorities are on his trail but even though this villain is no stereotypical "criminal genius", he's staying one or two steps ahead of one of the self-proclaimed "greatest police forces" in the world. All of a sudden, a woman calls in with a tip and the police narrow their search to the underground transit system. As luck would have it, two of the alleged "Finest" find themselves in a subway car with the spree-killing psychopath. All they have to do is make the arrest, bring the bad guy to justice, get a pat on the back from their Mayor and accept their keys to the city. But a funny thing happened on the way Fantasyland.

The killer, in full view of the "Finest", attacks an unarmed civilian who proceeds to defend himself and although he almost dies due to extreme negligence, he not only apprehends the killer, but disarms him and holds him until the "Finest" deem it safe to enter the scrum. The civilian survives, much to the chagrin of the "Finest" and he'll now go on to tell the world the truth. In spite of all this the city holds a ceremony to honor the civilian. How can this be?

It's very simple; the civilian wasn't honored by the city he helped rid of a killer. No, *that* city is doing their best to hide the truth of what really happened. The city that honored the civilian was the city of Philadelphia.

Exactly three months to the day of the incident, Philadelphia City Council honored me in a ceremony at Philadelphia City Hall. City Councilman Curtis Jones read the proclamation which included the following:

"WHEREAS, Mr. Lozito's brave response spared other innocent victims from similarly life threatening encounters; and

WHEREAS, Heroic acts like those taken by Mr. Lozito too often go underappreciated; now therefore

RESOLVED, BY THE COUNCIL OF THE CITY OF PHILADELPHIA, Hereby recognize and honor Joseph Lozito for his courageous actions in helping to detain an alleged serial killer in New York City.

FURTHER RESOLVED, That, an Engrossed copy of this resolution be presented to Mr. Lozito for his inspiring and exemplary actions, as evidence of the sincere sentiments of this legislative body.

As I've said numerous times, the city of Philadelphia is a great city. Honoring me like they did is really a thrill of a lifetime. I'm not one for politics or politicians, but this is a once-in-a-lifetime moment. Knowing all the issues any city has on their agenda, and to think a city would devote a few minutes to me, an adopted son, to recognize me for something I did in *another* city, is truly awe-inspiring. I will always look back at that day with immense pride. It makes me wonder what Philadelphia would do if a civilian stopped a killer in *their* city. One thing I doubt they do is turn their back on that person.

Squaring-off with "The Cupcake" Lloyd Woodard at Bellator 66

Chapter Twenty-One

I consider the information contained in the next few chapters to be a public service to all of you who plunked down your hard earned money to buy this book… thanks, by the way! I hope you all absorb what you're about to read. Everything you are about to read is a matter of public record and you can look it up for yourself if you have any doubts. You may have doubts because a lot of what you're about to read is truly unbelievable.

Our complaint was completed on January 17th, 2012 and was filed in the New York County Clerks Office on January 31st 2012. The reason why it took almost a year from the incident is because we couldn't file our complaint until the criminal portion of the incident was complete. Maksim Gelman decided to plead guilty and I'm thankful for that for two reasons. First, we would be able to move forward with the civil complaint without the delay of criminal trials and second, it meant I was that much closer to facing off with him again at his sentencing. More on that later.

I would imagine you understand at this point our reasons for filing the lawsuit. I'm sure I've repeated myself on several parts of it multiple times already so I'll mercifully refrain from doing it again. I will however quote from our complaint to give you the version of it in *"legalese"*.

Here are the key points of our complaint for you to digest:

9. *That upon information and belief, and at all times hereinafter mentioned, TERRANCE HOWELL (hereinafter "HOWELL") was and is a police officer in the* *employment of the defendants THE NEW YORK CITY POLICE DEPARTMENT, and/or NEW YORK CITY TRANSIT POLICE and/or THE CITY OF NEW YORK.*

10. *That upon information and belief and at all times hereinafter mentioned, HOWELL was acting within the scope of his employment with the defendants THE NEW YORK CITY POLICE DEPARTMENT and/or NEW YORK CITY TRANSIT POLICE and/or THE CITY OF NEW YORK.*

11. *That upon information and belief and at all times hereinafter mentioned, TAMARA TAYLOR (hereinafter "TAYLOR") was and is a police officer in the employment of the defendants THE NEW YORK CITY POLICE DEPARTMENT and/or NEW YORK CITY TRANSIT POLICE and/or THE CITY OF NEW YORK.*

12. *That upon information and belief and at all times hereinafter mentioned, TAYLOR was acting within the scope of her employment with the defendants THE NEW YORK CITY POLICE DEPARTMENT and/or NEW YORK CITY TRANSIT POLICE and/or THE CITY OF NEW YORK.*

13. *That on February 12,2011 at approximately 9:00 a.m. thereof HOWELL and TAYLOR were present on the first car of the "number three" New York City subway train.*

14. *That on the date and time aforesaid, HOWELL and TAYLOR were on said subway train for the purpose of searching for and apprehending an individual by the name of MAKSIM GELMAN (hereinafter "GELMAN").*

15. *GELMAN had committed four violent attacks resulting in the deaths of four individuals on February 11,2011.*

16. *That prior to the date and time aforesaid, HOWELL and TAYLOR were shown photographs of GELMAN in order to aid them in identifying him.*

17. *That on the date and time aforesaid, prior to the event complained of herein, GELMAN approached the conductor's compartment of the "number three" New York City subway train and falsely identified himself as a police officer to HOWELL and TAYLOR who were present therein in the course of their search for GELMAN.*

18. *That despite clearly visualizing GELMAN, and despite the knowledge of his violent propensities, HOWELL and TAYLOR failed to recognize GELMAN as the individual that they were seeking to locate and apprehend.*

19. *Prior to the events complained of herein, an individual who was a passenger in said subway car attempted to get the attention of HOWELL and TAYLOR while they were in the motorman's compartment for the purposes of notifying HOWELL and TAYLOR that GELMAN was on the subway train, and that said passenger's attempts were not recognized or acknowledged by officers HOWELL and TAYLOR.*

20. *That on or about February 12,2011 plaintiff was traveling on the New York number three New York City subway train when plaintiff was stabbed repeatedly by GELMAN.*

21. *That HOWELL and TAYLOR, while in close proximity to the plaintiff, observed plaintiff being attacked and, despite their knowledge of same, did not come to plaintiffs aide and instead remained in the closed motorman's car for their own safety.*

22. *That by reason of the facts set forth herein, a special relationship existed between defendants and the plaintiff.*

23. *That the aforesaid occurrence was caused by the negligence of the defendant in that, inter alia, defendants' employees and/or agents negligently failed to prevent* *the incident from occurring; failing to identify themselves as police officers to GELMAN; failed to draw their weapons and/or prevent in any way the actions of GELMAN; failing to properly and timely subdue GELMAN; failing to heed the warnings of fellow subway riders, of the presence of GELMAN; failing to recognize GELMAN as a dangerous fugitive posing an immediate risk to the plaintiff despite the fact that GELMAN approached officers TERRANCE HOWELL and TAMARA TAYLOR in the subway car prior to the attack; failing to timely come to the aide of claimant JOSEPH LOZITO; failing to mace and/or pepper spray and/or timely handcuff and/or otherwise subdue the assailant prior to or during the attack; failing to adequately, timely and properly provide medical attention for petitioner.*

24. *That the defendants created the dangerous conditions complained of herein and had notice of same and/or that the dangerous conditions complained of herein existed for a period of time prior to the occurrent that defendant, in its exercise of reasonable care, could have and should have had notice of the same.*

25. *That as a result of the defendant's negligence, plaintiff JOSEPH LOZITO, sustained severe and serious injuries; he has required and will continue to require medical aid and attention; he was incapacitated from his normal duties and was otherwise injured all to his damage in a sum of money that would exceed the jurisdictional limits of all lower courts which would otherwise have jurisdiction of this action.*

26. *That this action falls within one or more of the exceptions set forth in CPLR 5 1602.*

27. *Plaintiff ANDREA LOZITO repeats and realleges each and every allegation set forth in paragraphs "1" through "24" inclusive with the same force and effect as though herein set forth at length.*

28. *That at all times hereinafter mentioned plaintiff ANDREA LOZITO was and still is the spouse of the plaintiff JOSEPH LOZITO and resided with plaintiff.*

29. *That by reason of the foregoing plaintiff ANDREA LOZITO has been deprived of the services, society and consortium of the plaintiff JOSEPH LOZITO and as such has been deprived of love, companionship, affection, sexual relations, services, solace and other matrimonial relationships all to plaintiffs damages in the sum of money that would exceed the jurisdictional limits of all lower courts which would otherwise have jurisdiction of this action, together with the costs and disbursements of this action.*

WHEREFORE; the plaintiffs demand judgment against the defendants as follows:

(i) On the first cause of action herein in a sum of money that would exceed the jurisdictional limits of all lower courts which would otherwise have jurisdiction of this action;

(ii) On the second cause of action herein in a sum of money that would exceed the jurisdictional limits of all lower courts which would otherwise have jurisdiction of this action;

(iii) Together with the costs and disbursements of this action.

Whether you prefer the story coming from me in my own words or the more technical, legal format, I'm now going to use a term that both Joey and Dominic are fond of using. When it comes to the officer's in question....EPIC FAIL!

CHAPTER TWENTY-TWO

As you may imagine, when Corporation Counsel, the attorneys who represent New York City received our complaint, they didn't agree with it. In fact, they actually say that my injuries were *my fault!* That's right; it's *my fault* that I was attacked by a police-impersonating, spree-killing fugitive in full view of the *actual* police!

In their answer to our complaint, right on page one, they deny some allegations. Curious? I bet you are. Here are some of the allegations they **deny:**

"15. That on the date and time aforesaid, HOWELL and TAYLOR knew of the fact that GELMAN had committed four violent attacks resulting in the deaths of four individuals on February 11th, 2011" That's right, Officers Howell and Taylor were deployed to apprehend Maksim Gelman but ironically they had absolutely no idea why....hmmmm.

"17. That on the date and time aforesaid, prior to the event complained of herein, GELMAN approached the conductor's compartment of the "number three" New York City subway train and falsely identified himself as a police officer to HOWELL and TAYLOR who were present therein in the course of their search for GELMAN." See, now I'm really confused. Officer Howell told Gelman "you're not the Police" in response to.....*nothing?* Is Officer Howell psychic? Did he sense Gelman *"think"* he was a police officer *telepathically*, and if so, why couldn't he predict the attack?

"18. That despite clearly visualizing GELMAN, and despite the knowledge of his violent propensities, HOWELL and TAYLOR failed to recognize GELMAN as the individual that they were seeking to locate and apprehend." So are they saying that the officers DID recognize Gelman now? That's deplorable that they'd recognize him and still leave him in a subway car full of unarmed civilians.

"21. That HOWELL and TAYLOR, while in close proximity to the plaintiff, observed plaintiff being attacked and, despite their knowledge of same, did not come to plaintiffs aide and instead remained in the closed motorman's car for their own safety." Ok, ok, you got me on this one since I guess *technically* they did come out…eventually…once the threat was gone. Took them long enough, but I must admit, they did indeed come out.

Yes, all this and just on page one. Oh, it gets better. Here's page two where Corporation Counsel sets the record straight on just who exactly is to blame for the entire incident. Buckle up!

"6. Plaintiff(s)' culpable conduct caused or contributed, in whole or in part, to his/her/their injuries and or damages." Well since I'm the plaintiff they're referring to, I guess my injuries are my fault. Not Gelman's, not Howell's, not Taylor's… mine. What do the kids say nowadays, "my bad"?

This next point, I have to break up in sections, because honestly, it's priceless:

7. At all times mentioned in the complaint, plaintiff(s) knew or should have known in the exercise of due/reasonable care of the risks and dangers incident to engaging in the activity alleged. Plaintiff(s) voluntarily performed and engaged in the alleged activity and assumed the risk of the injuries and/or damages claimed. I guess they're right again since I did *voluntarily* defend myself against the killer they wanted absolutely no part of. Silly me, I didn't feel like dying that day. *Plaintiff(s) failed to use all required, proper, appropriate and reasonable safety devices and/or equipment and failed to take all proper, appropriate and reasonable steps to assure his/her/their safety.* Again, very valid point. I should have known where the "Killer Repellant Spray" was on the subway. I now know it is the box with the glass front that reads "In event of cowardly police, break glass!" *Plaintiff(s), primary assumption of risk solely caused his/her/their injuries and/or damage and defendant(s) owed no duty to the plaintiff(s) with respect to the risk assumed. Plaintiff(s), express assumption of risk solely caused his/her/their injuries and/or damage and defendant(s) owed no duty to the plaintiff(s) with respect to the risk assumed.* There you have it; the police owed no duty to protect, even when the killer they're looking for is less than twelve inches away. There I go again thinking the police are there to apprehend murderers. Will I ever learn? *Plaintiff(s), implied assumption of risk caused or contributed, in whole or in part to his/her/their injuries. In any action for injuries arising from the use of a vehicle in, or upon which plaintiff(s) were riding; it will be claimed that the injuries and/or damages sustained were caused by the failure of the plaintiff(s) to use available seat-belts and/or other safety devices.* That's right, I was almost hacked to death because I wasn't wearing a seat-belt nor did I utilize all the safety devices New York City provides on their subways. For the record, subways do not have seat-belts, nor do they have safety devices. Actually that day, some might consider the police "safety devices" but of course they'd be incorrect.

Go ahead; you know you need to read this again. There's no shame in it. I just wrote it and I need to read it again!

After Corporation Counsel submitted their reply to the Court, I asked Ed what would happen next. He explained that the next phase is called the "discovery" phase. During this part, attorneys gather as much evidence as possible about the situation. Many times, depositions are taken. During the discovery phase, both sides can obtain access to documents and evidence possessed by the other side. Ed told me we'd be very thorough in this phase and to expect the same from Corporation Counsel. Because of that, this portion could take several months to be completed. I had no problem with that at all. Ed also warned me that most likely, once the discovery phase was completed, to expect Corporation Counsel to submit a “Motion to Dismiss”. Unfortunately, he was wrong, Corporation Counsel wanted me to go away as quickly as possible and filed the aforementioned “Motion to Dismiss” even before we started the discovery phase. I wonder why?

Chapter Twenty-Three

From the very beginning, I was asked that when the case against Maksim Gelman would go to trial, would I testify against him? Are you kidding? Of course I would. I was looking forward to it and more than happy to do so. When Gelman decided to plead guilty, that took away any need for me, or anyone else for that matter to testify against him. All that was left now was his sentencing. Victims, or friends and family of victims would be allowed to make "impact statements" at sentencing. It's the opportunity to tell the judge, jury or the perp themselves just how the incident has affected you. You can also tell them what you think they deserve. Basically, I think as long as you keep it clean, you can say pretty much whatever you want. He'd be sentenced first in Brooklyn for the four murders and every attack other than myself. After that, he'd be sentenced in Manhattan for his cowardly attack on me.

On January 18th 2012, Gelman was sentenced in Brooklyn for all the charges except mine. Many times, criminals will display remorse or sorrow. They may try to explain the reasons for their heinous actions. They may even apologize in an attempt for forgiveness or leniency from a judge or jury. Gelman was having none of that. He was insulting, obnoxious and even had to be removed at one point for being so disruptive.

He mocked anyone and everyone that day from the victims, to their families and even the judge…at one point telling Judge Vincent Del Guidice to "suck his

Russian dick". He defamed the woman he was infatuated with, Yelena Bulchenko by calling her both a "heroin addict" and a "whore". When Bulchenko's boyfriend told Gelman he'd burn in hell, Gelman threatened to murder him as well. Gelman blamed everybody but himself. He blamed the victims for doing bad things for him. He blamed the police and DEA for not stopping him sooner. The line of the day came from Kenneth Taub, the chief of the Brooklyn district attorney's homicide bureau when he told the judge that Mr. Gelman "lacks a moral compass"...you think? Gelman was sentenced to 200 years in prison that day, a sentence most would agree isn't enough.

My day of reckoning would come a few weeks later on February 15th, 2012. I read his comments from his sentencing in Brooklyn and read how upset they made the families of the victims. I vowed things would be different when I had my say.

Full disclosure, I am not a genius. That being said, I hedged my bet that I'm smarter than Maks. He may be better at some things, like cowardly murdering defenseless women and older men or carjacking people and running people over, but he certainly wasn't smarter than me and was definitely not going to get the upper hand in either a war of words or a psychological confrontation.

I prepped myself by dumbing it down A LOT. I put myself in his head and thought about the things he might say to me. It wasn't too difficult. I figured he was too proud to admit that an unarmed man stopped him. I figured he'd tell me to perform fellatio on him. Maybe call me fat or bald; you know, real deep, intellectual insults. Probably act like an ass overall. I wasn't really going out on a limb there.

I made notes of things I wanted to say. I wanted to make sure to mention the names of the four people he murdered. I wanted him to hear them one last time. Not that I thought it'd make a difference, but I felt it needed to be done. I wanted to remind him of how I stopped him and maybe take a shot at him in the process. I wanted to mock him just as he'd mocked the families in Brooklyn. Most of all, I wanted him to know that even though he took his best shot at me, here I was, standing before him going on with my life while hoping he was well on his way to suffering even a fraction of the pain he dished out and then reminding him that he still had hell to look forward to. Yes, I was counting the days.

CHAPTER TWENTY-FOUR

The day that I was waiting for was finally here. I would get to face my attacker in the flesh. I had dreamed of our rematch. Sometimes we both had weapons; sometimes it was just hand-to-hand combat. Never once did I have a weapon and him not. Probably because I'm not a coward like that. Sometimes we were on the subway, on the street, in a cage, in a ring and sometimes we were in a room without windows. It was always violent and I always felt better afterwards. Today would be a little different but I was hopeful it would be just as satisfying.

I have a great family. They wanted to come to court to support me but I asked them not to. I was on my own the first time we squared off and I wanted to be alone this time. I also knew if any of them went, it would be very emotional for them. I know I can handle Gelman saying stupid shit about me, but it would have sent me over the edge had he said anything to a family member. I knew I'd be ok and although I was met with resistance from several family members, they all complied with my wishes.

I would not be alone that day though. My boss Pete and co-worker Nat Francisco asked if they could attend and although I wanted to be alone, I knew those two attending would be very different than if Andrea, my mom or a sibling were in attendance. Also a buddy of mine Bauzen wanted to film a piece for the Middle Easy website so he was there as well.

I met with A.D.A. Linn and he went through what was about to happen. He asked if I wanted him to view my statement but I politely declined. I was going to say what *I* wanted to say and how *I* wanted to say it. We made our way to the courtroom and then it was just a waiting game. Pete and Nat were there already so I took a seat with them. I believe we had very little conversation as I was preparing for psychological warfare.

I didn't know how this whole thing worked. I was a courtroom full of people who were there for various reasons and various indiscretions. I would consider them the "undercard" to Gelman and my "main event". Throughout all these other cases, there was exactly one court officer present. Suddenly, there was a long pause after a case and three or four more court officers arrived on the scene. They congregated around the perp table like a football huddle and when they "broke" the biggest one came over by me and the rest of them stayed by the table. A podium was set up so I started to put two and two together and figured "showtime" wasn't far off!

A door in the front of the courtroom opened and in walked a shackled Maksim Gelman. As was the case in Brooklyn, not a single friend or family member was there to support him but I'm guessing it was for slightly different reasons than why I asked *my* family not to attend. He looked a little heavier than he did during our first encounter. I'm not sure if it had anything to do with his super-awesome new orange jumpsuit or not, but he looked a tad bulkier. He also sported a bandage above his right eye. Not sure what happened there. Maybe he demanded someone suck his dick again and they objected? Who knows? It was a good look for him though.

Without even realizing it, when he entered the courtroom, I immediately shot up out of my seat. The burly court officer looked at me and instructed me to sit down. At that point is when I realized I was actually standing up. I sat down but never took my eyes off the invertebrate.

A.D.A. Linn made a presentation to Judge Richard Carruthers which I would imagine is standard stuff for this type of situation. I admit, I rolled my eyes and giggled a little when Linn stated New York City's standard line of bullshit that I *helped* Officers Howell and Taylor. For a moment, I contemplated correcting him since I knew several media outlets were there covering it, but I took the high road and figured anyone who heard him say that knew it was a load of garbage. This was neither the time nor the place. This was about getting human scum off the street for the rest of his miserable life.

I was prompted to approach the podium and I did. My heart was racing. I had so much to say and I wanted to make sure I said it all. I should have kept my notes so I could be 100% accurate, but this was a good day for me so I'm pretty sure I remember it all.

Me-"Your Honor, I do not wish to take up much of the courts time as this guy here has a lot of time *he* has to start serving. I don't want to keep him here any longer than I have to.

First, I'd like to thank Alfred Douglas for saving my life that day. (Looking over at Gelman) I've waited over a year to look into those eyes again to see the soul of a coward. When you attacked me and I took you down, you went down real easy"

Gelman-"You didn't take me down, you jerkoff"

Me-What did you say you moron? Ladies and gentlemen, what we have here is the funniest Russian since Yakov Smirnoff. I appreciate that you chose me, I really do. Maybe if you'd continued your extreme cowardice, you would have picked on another person, a woman and maybe she couldn't defend herself. Or a child?"

Gelman-"fucking moron...jerkoff"

Me-"Why are you so angry?"

Gelman-"I'm not angry"

Me-"Just think about the lives you have changed, Alexander Kusnetsov, Anna Bulchenko, Yelena Bulchenko, Steven Tannenbaum. They'll never get to walk the face of this earth again because you're a spoiled little boy who nobody listened to as a kid. Instead of taking your ball and going home, you threw a tantrum. Well, I wish you all the best. I hope you rot in your cell and you have hell to look forward to, so enjoy it."

Gelman-"That jerk off can suck my dick"

Me-"No thank you, for the record"

Gelman-""The only thing I have to say is Kim Kardashian, will you marry me? I'll make it last more than seventy-two days."

With that, Supreme Court Justice Richard Carruthers added twenty-five more years to the 200 years Gelman had already been sentenced to in Brooklyn.

It was a liberating experience. So therapeutic. I thought to myself that if I could do that once a month, it would go a long way in the healing process. I met with reporters for a few minutes after the sentencing then Pete, Nat, Bauzen and myself made our way to a restaurant for a few beers and some Chicken Parmigiana.

CHAPTER TWENTY-FIVE

With the first evil, Gelman, now in jail for the rest of his life, it was time to turn all my attention the second evil, Corporation Counsel. Psychology may say that Gelman was born like that. Maybe elements from his childhood contributed to his twisted way of way life. Some may argue without the proper intervention at a younger age, he didn't have a choice, that he was *destined* to be evil. Now I believe that indeed, some people are just born that way and also some people become that way, either by choice or circumstance. In my opinion, defense attorneys are evil. To willingly defend people who have committed some of the most disgusting, inhumane acts is deplorable. To me, what Michael Gibek and Corporation Counsel did in defending Howell and Taylor is similar to defending criminals. They'll argue they were just doing their jobs, the same lament often stated by defense attorneys.

Don't misunderstand; I completely understand the role of Corporation Counsel in this. Two of their officers "shit the bed" on February 12th, 2011 and it was their job to make it go away. I also completely understand that whether they'd admit it or not, not a single person on the side of New York City wanted ANYTHING to do with a trial. I'd imagine we'd hear the standard nonsense about tax dollars or backlogged cases but I call bullshit. All I ever wanted was to square off, Glory World Series style in a court of law against Howell and Taylor. I wanted Tim Hughes in the center of the courtroom handling the introductions...asking the jury "Are you readdyyy?" All I ever wanted was my truth against their truth to be judged by a jury of my peers. I've stated on the record that had a jury decided against me, I would have washed my hands of the whole thing. The judicial process would have been at work and even if it didn't work in my favor, so be it. Unfortunately, the Evil Empire that is Corporation Counsel didn't need trickery or black magic to make it go away; they just twisted the law with an inane loophole.

The old expression "you can't fight City Hall" has its merits. Ed Chakmakian is very good at what he does so when I received a call from him telling me that he had racked his brains trying to come up with a response to the Corporation Counsel's motion to dismiss as well as enlisting the services of several of his colleagues to no avail, I was devastated. He asked to be recused from the case so I could explore other options but still offered to help in any way possible. I asked what my options were and it seemed they were limited. I could attempt to find another lawyer but time would have been an issue with that as asking for another adjournment surely would not be welcomed by the court. I could drop the case, which really was never an option. I then asked Ed if I could continue on my own, *pro se?* Of course I didn't use the phrase "pro se" in our conversation. The first time I'd heard it was when Ed said it to me. Ed was brutally honest with me and told me that the way this case was going, I really didn't have anything to lose, but also to be prepared for anything, up to and including dismissal. Right then and there I decided I would continue the fight. Abraham Lincoln once said "he who represents himself has a fool for a client". He may be right, but at this point, I felt it was my best course of action. Heck, the NYPD left me to battle Gelman on my own, why not battle New York City singlehandedly?

I did not have much time to prepare my response. Ed advised me to show up on the date assigned and ask for an adjournment based on me now representing myself. I showed up that day and I was nervous as hell. Talk about anxiety! Here I am going before the court asking for one more adjournment when I know they won't be thrilled. There were two gentlemen in the court that day. They had the "good-cop-bad-cop" thing down pat. One guy was very nice and professional. The other was as nasty as could be. Of course it was the nasty one that I had to ask for the adjournment. To say he wasn't pleased would be an understatement but he reluctantly gave me a little more time. I did appreciate that, although I could have done without the bullying tactics. It's a shame when two adult men can't just have a conversation but who knows, maybe he didn't like my face?

I took my time going over their motion and read it several times. Corporation Counsel's main argument was that "no special relationship existed" between the police and myself, therefore for me to expect Officers Howell and Taylor to take police action was unreasonable. Really? OK, I'll play along. They went on to cite several examples of cases that were thrown out where it was *"proven"* the special relationship didn't exist. As you'll soon read, they bear no resemblance at all to my situation.

I put every ounce of energy into this and quite frankly, I think for a non-lawyer, it's pretty damn good. I went at it straight-forward, as a layman, and tried to use common sense. That may have been my first mistake. Before I take you through the cases, just in case you haven't visited the NYPD's official website lately, I'd like to bring a few things to your attention. Take a look at the "Mission" section of the website and you'll find the following:

MISSION-*The MISSION of the New York City Police Department is to enhance the quality of life in our City by working in partnership with the community and in accordance with constitutional rights to enforce the laws, preserve the peace, reduce fear, and provide for a safe environment.*

My question is, the officers on the train knew why they were looking for Maksim Gelman. He murdered four people and injured several others. How were they "reducing fear" and "providing a safe environment" by ignoring the murderer they were looking for and leaving him in a subway car full of men, women and children?

VALUES-*IN PARTNERSHIP WITH THE COMMUNITY, WE PLEDGE TO:*

- *Protect the lives and property of our fellow citizens and impartially enforce the law.*

- *Fight crime both by preventing it and by aggressively pursuing violators of the law.*
- *Maintain a higher standard of integrity than is generally expected of others because so much is expected of us.*
- *Value human life, respect the dignity of each individual and render our services with courtesy and civility.*

On February 12th, 2011, Officers Howell and Taylor did the exact opposite of all the *Values* listed on the New York City Police Department website. By not acting in a timely manner to take police action, to confront and apprehend Maksim Gelman after Mr. Gelman identified himself as a police officer, the officers DID NOT:

"Protect the lives and property of our fellow citizens and impartially enforce the law." No protection at all was offered. The officers were made aware by the fugitive himself that he was in the very car they occupied, yet they didn't take any action until said fugitive had attacked a passenger. They had ample time between Mr. Gelman announcing his presence with authority and the subsequent altercation that ensued to take action.

"Fight crime both by preventing it and by aggressively pursuing violators of the law." Officers Howell and Taylor were the opposite of "aggressive" that day, they were as "passive" as possible. Had they been even the slightest bit aggressive, none of us would be in this situation right now.

"Maintain a higher standard of integrity than is generally expected of others because so much is expected of us." Their timidity in relation to Mr. Gelman, in spite of being armed and outnumbering him, tells one all they need to know about their integrity and how much the general public mean to them.

"Value human life, respect the dignity of each individual and render our services with courtesy and civility." By knowingly allowing an alleged spree-killer to occupy the same area as men, women and children, Officers Howell and Taylor displayed a total lack of respect and absolutely no value of human life. By leaving the public with a man who had already taken four lives, how can they value any other human life other than the ones they chose to save, their own?

On August 25th, 2012 an article appeared in the New York Times **(After Bystanders Take Bullets, Questions on Police Protocol by Michael Wilson)** concerning the excessive use of force by the New York Police Department in the case where Jeffrey T. Johnson had allegedly murdered a former co-worker, Steven Ercolino, and then pointed his gun at police. The police fired at Johnson, killing him on the spot, but also injured nine innocent bystanders in the midst of the gunfire. *Geoffrey P. Alpert, a criminologist at the University of South Carolina and an expert on the police use of force, said that hitting innocent civilians "doesn't happen very often, but it happens." He added: "The rule of thumb is that you do not put civilians in the line of fire, but the rule of thumb is also that you don't let a murderer get away."* My question is, does this "rule of thumb" only apply to crimes committed by murderers above ground? I ask because Officers Howell & Taylor did absolutely nothing to stop Maksim Gelman from getting away. The reality is, when Mr. Gelman walked away from the door after identifying himself as a police officer, he could have very well kept walking into other cars and potentially leave the train at a future stop.

On October 25*th* , 2012 an article appeared in the New York Daily News, **(NYPD Officer Gilberto Valle arrested by FBI over failed plot to kidnap women and cook them by Rocco Parascandola and Greg B. Smith).** In this article, a quote is attributed to Manhattan U.S. Attorney Preet Bharara that states *"This case is all the more disturbing when you consider Valle's position as a New York City police officer and his sworn duty to serve and protect".* Quotes like these are spoken daily, and they are dramatic. They are also the truth. The men and women who graduate the Police Academy and are promoted to police officers indeed take an oath to "serve and protect". Yet when members of "New York's Finest" fail miserably and are called on the carpet, Corporation Counsel allows them to hide behind loopholes in the law that are in direct contrast to the very same oath taken when they are sworn in. How can both be correct?

Chapter Twenty-Six

I'd advise you to sit down for this chapter. Not only is it the longest in the book, but what I'm about to present to you are the cases that Corporation Counsel used to get my case dismissed. Some of these cases are horrible. Some of these cases are tragic. Some of these cases are downright silly. They all have one thing in common, they have zero to do with what happened to me on the train. All are cases you can look up with a simple internet search if you think I'm lying. So, without further ado, I present to you "fluff, fluff and more fluff". Take it away Michael Gibek!

The case of Castle Rock v. Gonzales is apparently the "go-to" case in instances like these for Corporation Counsel. This is a truly horrifying and heartbreaking case. Castle Rock, Colorado resident Jessica Gonzales, during divorce proceedings, obtained a restraining order against her husband on June 4th, 1999, requiring him to remain at least one-hundred yards from her and their three daughters except during specified visitation time. On June 22nd at approximately 5:15 pm, her husband took possession of the three children in violation of the order. Gonzales called the police at approximately 7:30 pm, 8:30 pm, 10:10 pm, and 12:15 am on June 23rd, and also visited the police station in person at 12:40 am on June 23rd, 1999. However, since Ms. Gonzales from time to time, did allow her husband to take the children at various hours, the police took no action despite the husband having called Gonzales prior to her second call to the police and informing her that he had the children with him at an amusement park in Denver, Colorado. At approximately 3:20 am on June 23rd, 1999, the husband appeared at the Castle Rock police station and instigated a fatal shoot-out with the police. A search of his vehicle revealed the corpses of the three daughters, whom the husband had killed prior to his arrival. He died afterwards. This case is a tragedy on several levels, but in my opinion, a restraining order case has nothing to do with my case. In the above case, the police were not mere feet away from the father as he killed his children as Officers Howell and Taylor were as Mr. Gelman attempted to murder me nor did I have a restraining order against Mr. Gelman.

In Cuffy v. City of New York, the plaintiffs contacted the police and alerted them of threats by their neighbor and wanted said neighbor to be arrested. Mr. Cuffy was told by authorities that they would arrest the neighbor in the morning. The next morning, the neighbor was never arrested and several members of the Cuffy family were attacked later that evening. In this instance, Mr. Cuffy's neighbor was not a police impersonating, spree-killing fugitive on the run from the law and the police were not in a physical position to apprehend the neighbor in the moments immediately prior to the attacks.

In the case of Valdez v. City of New York, we again have an order of protection instance. In July 1996, Carmen Valdez obtained an order of protection against her ex-boyfriend, Felix Perez, who had assaulted and stalked her. The order, Valdez' second against Perez, barred Perez from contacting Valdez. One week later, Valdez testified at trial and Perez called Valdez and threatened to kill her. Valdez left her apartment with her twin five-year-old sons and used a payphone to call the police officer handling her case. The officer, Valdez testified, told her to return to her apartment "immediately," and said Perez would be found quickly and arrested. The next day, Perez showed up at Valdez' apartment and shot her multiple times, seriously injuring her before killing himself. This case is another tragic instance and my heart goes out to Carmen Valdez and her family. That being said, unless the officers in question were inside Valdez' apartment at the time of the attack specifically looking for Felix Perez, I again fail to see the relevance in using this case to aid in a dismissal.

In the case of Kircher v. City of Jamestown, Plaintiff Deborah Kircher was forced into her own car, driven to a remote area and brutally beaten and raped. Two persons observed the abduction, attempted unsuccessfully to intervene, and gave chase in their own vehicle. When the witnesses lost sight of the other car, they stopped and reported the incident to a City of Jamestown police officer. The officer said he would report the matter, but apparently did not. Plaintiff sought to hold the officer and the city liable for their failure to respond to the witnesses' report. Once again, we have an extremely horrific case and I cannot imagine what that must have been like for Deborah Kircher, but once again, unless the officers were two or three feet away from Brian Blanco when he abducted Kircher and chose to do absolutely nothing to prevent the incident, I fail to see any relevance in citing this case.

In the case of Bonner v. City of New York, the Court of Appeals held that the city was acting in its governmental and not proprietary capacity when it failed to fix a broken gate at a schoolyard where a teacher was assaulted by a third party. Once again, unless the police were present and in position to apprehend the assailant, I fail to see any relevance in citing this case.

In the case of Marilyn S. vs. City of New York, the plaintiff Marilyn S. a school teacher at a New York City high school, was sexually assaulted in the faculty ladies' room by a male intruder on December 7th, 1981. The room was ordinarily kept locked and the plaintiff entered it by using her own key. The assailant was never apprehended and there was no evidence as to how he had entered the second-story windowless room. At trial, the plaintiffs sought to establish that Marilyn S.'s injuries had been proximately caused by the defendants' negligent failure, in their proprietary capacity as landlords to maintain their premises in a reasonably safe condition. Specifically, the plaintiffs alleged that the defendants had maintained a system of distributing keys that was so inadequate and disorganized that keys were likely to fall into unauthorized hands, thereby making it foreseeable that such a violent intrusion and injury would occur. Another horrible case in which the plaintiffs life was changed forever. I fail to see any similarities between my case and this one, other than myself and Marilyn S. are humans and we both brought action against the City of New York.

In the case of Yearwood v. Town of Brighton, the Town of Brighton police investigated a domestic quarrel and left after advising plaintiff, Ingrid Yearwood that they could neither arrest her estranged husband, who had threatened to kill her, nor remove her children from the family home which he had threatened to burn. Several hours later, her two sons, ages 3 and 7, died in a fire set in their home by the estranged husband. Yet another tragedy, just senseless and horrible. I did not read anywhere in the case the part where the police were present when Yearwood's estranged husband started the fire. The reason is, they weren't. Again, no relevance to my case. Completely different circumstances.

In the case of Vitale v. City of New York, Plaintiff Peter Vitale, an industrial arts teacher at a junior high school, was injured when he was assaulted by a student as he sought to break up an altercation in the hallway of the school. Once again, unless the assailant was a police impersonating, spree-killing fugitive on the run from the law and the police were in a physical position to apprehend the assailant in the moments immediately prior to the attack, I do not see the connection between my case and this one.

In the case of Weiner v. Metropolitan Transp. Auth., the courts ruled that the New York City Transit Authority owes no duty to protect a person on its premises from assault by a third party, absent facts establishing a special relationship between the authority and the person assaulted. Ann Weiner was assaulted by a man with a knife, just like I was, but the similarities end there. Her assailant was not a police impersonating, spree-killing fugitive on the run from the law and the police were not in a physical position to apprehend said assailant in the moments immediately prior to the attack.

In the case of Riss v. City of New York, Plaintiff was harassed by a rejected suitor, who claimed he would kill or seriously injure her if she dated someone else. Plaintiff repeatedly asked for police protection and was ignored. After the news of her engagement, the plaintiff was again threatened and called the police to no avail. The next day, a thug, sent by the rejected suitor, partially blinded the plaintiff and disfigured her face. The pattern of tragic cases cited by Corporation Counsel continues, but also continuing is the pattern of the tragic events happening while the police were not present. The police were not two to three feet away when Riss was attacked like Officers Howell and Taylor were when I was attacked.

In the case of Besedina v. New York City Transit Authority and City, Maria Besedina was raped twice on the subway platform of the 21st Street subway station in Queens by an assailant who had followed her off a "G" train. Her claim against the New York City Transit Authority and the Metropolitan Transportation Authority is premised largely on the failure of the employees of the Transit Authority to come to her aid. In this case, the city employee in question was a transit worker, NOT a New York City Police Officer. I call into question the transit workers integrity if he could have watched a woman getting raped and not do anything, but the worker was NOT a uniformed and armed member of the New York City Police Department. I do not see the connection between my case and this one.

In the case of Finch v. County of Saratoga, Vincent Finch filed suit against the County of Saratoga, seeking to recover for injuries sustained when he was shot by Bruce Mosher in the Town of Corinth, Saratoga County, on December 22nd, 1995. Finch's theory of the case was that the defendant— more specifically, the

Saratoga County Sheriff's Department— failed to adequately protect plaintiff from Mosher despite being advised on a number of occasions that Mosher was stalking and harassing him. Beginning to notice a pattern? Once again, we have a case where the police were nowhere near the incident when it happened. Not a single member of the Saratoga County Sheriff's Department watched as Mosher shot Finch. Again, completely different situation than when Officer's Howell and Taylor stood by and watched Maksim Gelman attack me.

In the case of Gallogly v. Village of Mohawk, John Gallogly alleged an assault perpetrated on him by a third person in plain view of a police officer of defendant village. Here we have a case that while *somewhat* similar to mine, is indeed quite different. While the officers in question have similar intestinal fortitude to Officers Howell and Taylor, the Village of Mohawk Officers were not specifically looking for a police impersonating, spree-killing fugitive on the run from the law. Similar, yes, but the circumstances surrounding my attack would make even the Village of Mohawk officers embarrassed to be associated with Officers Howell and Taylor. While there are similarities between the two cases, the differences far outweigh those similarities.

In the case of Rodriguez v. City of New York, On March 4th, 1984, Mariano Rodriguez was an innocent passerby during a shootout between the police and Ramon Flores. The incident began when a group pursued Mr. Flores south on Jerome Avenue, throwing bottles and garbage cans at him. A crowd was attracted by the commotion and at some point Flores drew a gun and began firing at his assailants. Prior to the incident, plaintiff Mariano Rodriguez had been in a hardware store on the west side of Jerome Avenue. He crossed the street to the east side. He recalled seeing a lot of people "screaming and yelling and running", but heard no shots and saw no one with a gun at any time. He ran straight across the street toward the statue store. He was shot and he felt a burning pain upon approaching the west sidewalk. This seems like a case that Corporation Counsel would cite when the unlucky nine that were wounded by police at the Empire State Building file lawsuits. Once again, absolutely nothing to do with my case.

In Liebowitz v. Bank Leumi Trust Co. of New York, the plaintiff alleges that she commenced her employment with the defendant Bank Leumi Trust Company of New York in April 1981 as a junior collector in the collections department, and that the individual defendants Hahn and Hurley were her supervisors throughout the entire period of her employment. Although the plaintiff assertedly "had an outstanding work record" and "commanded the respect of her fellow workers and peers", she alleges that she was "repeatedly denied promotions that others less qualified received", owing to the fact that she is "a Jewish female". I honestly have no idea where to begin with this one.

In AG Capital Funding Partners, L.P. v. State St. Bank & Trust Co., I can't even type this one with a straight face. I never went to law school, but this is a financial case that doesn't involve New York City Police Officers watching a man they are charged with apprehending stabbing an innocent bystander. With all due respect, the only similarity between my case and this one is the "v." in the middle.

Nonnon v. City of New York is about contaminated water potentially causing diseases. Pace v. Perk is about fraud. Jacobson v. Chase Manhattan Bank N.A. is about a man, an exotic car and a credit card. Alvarez v. Prospect Hospital is a medical malpractice case. In Zuckerman v. City of New York, Muriel Zuckerman fell at a curb while attempting to board a bus. Mallad Construction Corp. v County Federal Savings & Loan Assoc. is about breach of a financing contract. Tobron Office Furniture Corporation v. King World Productions, Inc. is about partial delivery of furniture. Polanco v. City of New York dealt with Mr. Polanco's car being hit with a New York City Sanitation truck. In Judith M. v. Sisters of Charity Hospital, plaintiff alleges that a hospital employee sexually abused her while she was an inpatient at Sisters of Charity Hospital. Brill v. City of New York dealt with Mrs. Brill tripping and falling on a New York City sidewalk. In Blackstock v. Board of Education of the City of New York, we, once again, have a teacher attacked by a student.

In Garcia v. O'Keefe, this case deals with false arrest. Kudos to the officers for being active, unlike Officer's Howell and Taylor. In Mahase v. Manhattan & Bronx Surface Transit Operating Auth., we have a slip & fall case. Plaintiff in this case did not slip over a murderer, nor did plaintiff slip over two sedentary police officers who were watching the incident. In Mazzilli v. City of New York, plaintiff Mazzilli was assaulted by New York City Police Officers. Officers Howell and Taylor would have had to take action to potentially assault me, or anyone else on the train for that matter. No action taken by the officers actually led to the only assault, which was Gelman assaulting me. In Pulka v. Edelman, this case involves a parking garage and an injury to a pedestrian struck by a car while it was being driven out of the garage and across an adjacent sidewalk, not by a garage employee, but by a patron of the garage. Of course, no connection to my case.

In Rollins v. Board of Education of the City of New York, Maria Rollins, a school safety officer, filed a claim for negligent failure to protect her from injury caused by a student. Another case of a school employee being injured by a student. Another case of the student not being a police impersonating, spree-killing fugitive on the run from the law and the police were not in a physical position to apprehend the student in the moments immediately prior to the attacks.

In Lauer v. City of New York, a father was named the prime suspect in the tragic death of his son based on a medical examiner's report stating the cause of death as homicide. It was later discovered that the boy died of an aneurysm. Relevance to my case? That's correct, none.

In McPherson v. New York City Housing Authority, Donna McPherson, a tenant in a public housing project owned by the defendant, suffered multiple gunshot wounds as she was sitting on a bench located outside of her building. No police were on the scene at the time of the shooting. Police were at the scene when I was attacked on the subway by Maksim Gelman. Similar? Not at all.

In Gonzalez v. New York City Housing Authority, plaintiff brought a wrongful death action against the New York City Housing Authority when their grandmother was brutally attacked & murdered in her apartment. Again, uniformed and armed police were not present when she was attacked. This case is not in any way, shape or form similar to mine.

In Barksdale v. New York City Transit Authority, Plaintiff's decedent died when she fell from a moving subway train in an attempt to change cars. Plaintiff alleged in her Notice of Claim to the New York City Transit Authority, dated September 4th, 1990, that her decedent's death was caused by the Authority's negligence, which consisted of: "failing to properly maintain the guard chains between trains, the railings between trains and properly safeguard the passengers so that when decedent was forced to go from one train to the other due to being molested by other passengers, she fell from the train because the chains were not in place and were defective." Well, at least this case involves a subway, as does mine. Unfortunately, I don't see the part about uniformed and armed police officers watching a spree-killing, police impersonating fugitive chasing the plaintiff's decedent.

In Gonzalez v. Pius, The infant plaintiff suffered second and third degree burns over approximately 15% of her face, shoulder, scalp, neck and wrist as a result of a kitchen accident in which she was scalded with hot oil from an electric frying pan which her mother had been using. The accident occurred when the infant came in contact with a portion of the electric wire leading to the frying pan. The plaintiff alleged that the failure of the appellants to install a stove in the apartment where the infant was residing with her mother forced the mother to resort to alternative and potentially more hazardous methods of cooking food. Horrible, horrible incident, but once again, nothing in common with my case.

In Pelaez v. Seide, this case involves child injuries due to exposure to lead paint. I hate cases where children become ill. Most people probably feel the same. While the Pelaez family has my sympathies, I must admit to not seeing the connection between this case and mine.

In Abraham v. City of New York, this case dealt with students and teachers of Our Lady of Lourdes school becoming infected with active tuberculosis by a teacher. Nothing here about cops watching as the killer they're looking for was attempting to add another notch to his "murderer's belt".

In Fisher v. Giuca, On October 11th, 2003, Michael Fisher's son was shot and killed. Two men, John Giuca and Antonio Russo, were convicted of the murder. The plaintiffs commenced action to recover damages for wrongful death and negligence against, among others, Giuca and Russo, the decedent's friend, Angel DiPietro, and DiPietro's friend, Al Cleary. I read the complaint and did not see where officers were in pursuit of Giuca and Russo and then watched as they killed Fisher. That's because it didn't happen that way.

In Mon v. City, the lawsuit arises out of events which occurred in the Bronx on August 21st, 1982 near the intersection of Brady and Holland Avenues following an altercation between defendant Shankman and plaintiffs, Andre Mon and his brother, Rodney Mon. Shankman, a recently appointed police officer, while off-duty, shot his service revolver twice, hitting both plaintiffs and injuring Andre Mon seriously. Plaintiffs were arrested but all charges against Andre Mon were dismissed and the charge against Rodney Mon resulted in acquittal. Their damage claims against the city for false arrest and for personal injuries on the theory of negligent hiring were tried together before a jury. Here we have a case of an aggressive off-duty police officer shooting two individuals. In my case, we have two passive police officers watching the man they're looking for assault me. The only similarity between the cases is that the numbers add up to three.

In Grieshaber v. City of Albany, this action arises out of the tragic death of Jenna Grieshaber Honis, who was murdered in her basement apartment in the City of Albany on the evening of November 6th, 1997. The theory of the complaint is that defendant was negligent in its response to an emergency 911 telephone call that decedent made at 6:47 pm on that day. Although police officers arrived at decedent's apartment building at 6:52 pm, they awaited the arrival of an animal control officer to subdue decedent's dog. As a result, they did not actually enter decedent's apartment until approximately 7:45 pm, at which time they found her lying on the floor with a bedpost of a heavy wooden bed resting on her neck. Decedent was ultimately transported to a nearby hospital emergency room, where she was pronounced dead at 8:31 pm. The autopsy report indicates that the cause of death was asphyxiation due to compression of decedent's neck. This case would be similar, except that the Albany police would have needed to witness the assault and have watched as she was killed. Again, no similarity.

In Dinardo v. City of New York, Plaintiff Zelinda DiNardo, a special education teacher at a New York City public school, was injured when she tried to restrain one student from attacking another. I think we've covered this in similar cases earlier in this chapter. In Tango v. Tulevech, this case involves child visitation and custody. Nothing to do with police dereliction of duty. Kelleher v. Town of Southampton, deals with coastal erosion, denial of an application and subsequent damages to beach house. Rottkamp v. Young deals with zoning issues and the construction of a diner. In Green v. City of New York, this action was filed to recover damages for negligent interference with plaintiff's common-law right to possession of her deceased son's body. McLean v. City, has to do with safety in a person's home that was being used as a child-care facility. Pandolfo v. U.A. Cable

Systems of Watertown, this case involves theft of cable television services. Coyne v. State involves an underage drinker becoming intoxicated and wandering onto a state highway and dying after being struck by a vehicle.

In Miller v. State, Appellant Odie Miller was convicted of robbery while armed with a deadly weapon, a class B felony, Ind. Code § 35-42-5-1 (Burns 1979 Repl.). The trial court imposed a prison term of thirteen years. Appellant raises three issues in this direct appeal: (1) Whether evidence of a third party's extrajudicial statement identifying the perpetrator by name constituted inadmissible hearsay; (2) Whether evidence identifying him as the perpetrator is sufficient, and (3) Whether a screwdriver constitutes a "deadly weapon" for purposes of the robbery statute. I would like to raise another issue, if I may? What does this case have to do with mine?

In Estate of Scheuer v. City of New York, Plaintiffs maintain that their 91-year-old decedent wandered from her apartment after her home health care aide left for the evening and that it was not until almost three weeks later, after an unsuccessful search by the NYPD of the decedent's apartment complex, that the decedent was found by a management employee in an unlocked, vacant apartment two floors directly below her apartment. An autopsy determined that a heart attack was the cause of death. Plaintiffs allege the NYPD's search of the vacant apartments was negligent and that such negligence caused the decedent pain and suffering and ultimately, her death. While I would say that the police in question could have searched a little more in detail based on where the woman was eventually found, once again, this case has nothing to do with mine. Completely different circumstances.

In Nash v. City of New York, Plaintiffs sought damages for emotional distress arising from the city's purportedly negligent missing person investigation for their deceased adult son, a Connecticut resident reported missing in early November 1997.

Decedent's unidentified body was found in the water near Pier 5 in Brooklyn within two weeks of his disappearance. Decedent was not identified until approximately eleven months later, apparently as a result of a computer database entry error. Again, nothing to do with my case.

In McCormack v. City of New York, Plaintiff's wrongful death claim against New York City arose out of an incident in which an Emergency Services Unit (ESU) police officer was shot and killed when an apparently emotionally disturbed individual who had barricaded himself inside a house emerged and fired a shotgun directly at him. Plaintiff's claim was premised on two distinct theories. First, plaintiff alleged that the city was negligent in supplying the decedent with a bullet-proof vest called a "Davis vest" that was not fit for use in situations involving barricaded, armed individuals, because unlike some newer body armor equipment, the Davis vest left the wearer's sides exposed. Second, plaintiff contended that a negligently issued order from one of the commanding officers directing the ESU team members not to fire at the barricaded individual, even if he discharged his weapon, was the proximate cause of the decedent's death. Not the same. The police were not looking for this man prior to the incident. The police did not have ample opportunity to apprehend this man prior to the incident. Two things Officers Howell and Taylor cannot say.

In Coleman v. Corporate Loss Prevention Asso., The plaintiff was arrested for trademark counterfeiting in connection with Kim's Specialty Store after an investigation by the defendant, a private investigation firm, led to the discovery of merchandise from the store with counterfeit labels. Pursuant to a plea agreement, the plaintiff's girlfriend, an owner of the store, pleaded guilty to a misdemeanor charge of trademark counterfeiting, and the charges against the plaintiff were adjourned in contemplation of dismissal. Thereafter, the plaintiff commenced this action against the defendant for negligent investigation and supervision, claiming that he was not an owner, employee, or agent of the store. Once again, nothing to do with my case.

Still with me? I do apologize for the length of this chapter but I felt you needed to see what Corporation Counsel presented to the court. I hope you're as infuriated as I was upon reading this!

Chapter Twenty-Seven

Interestingly enough, one case Corporation Counsel did not cite was Dorsett vs. County of Nassau, 800 F.Supp.2d 453 (2011). This is but one case where the "special relationship" criteria didn't absolve and didn't protect abysmal police work. Many cases cited in Corporation Counsel's motion are those dealing with orders of protection. In this case, in 2009, Sharon Dorsett's daughter, Jo'Anna Bird was brutally murdered by her estranged boyfriend and father of her two children, Leonardo Valdez-Cruz. Several attempts were made by Bird to end their relationship when finally Valdez-Cruz stabbed Ms. Bird so many times, including in her eyes, that the medical examiner was unable to count the wounds. Valdez-Cruz is now living the rest of his miserable life in prison for among other things, first-degree murder by torture.

Sharon Dorsett sued Nassau County alleging officers repeatedly ignored protective orders shielding Bird from Valdez-Cruz, refusing to arrest him for violating those orders. This suit was settled, out of court for 7.7 million dollars. Why wouldn't counsel for Nassau County invoke a defense as Corporation Counsel has in my case and attempt to get her case dismissed if this was so black and white? It's because it is not that simple. I find Corporation Counsel's attempt to dismiss my case as a personal insult. My feeling is, had a relative of Michael Gibek been on that #3 train the morning of February 12th, 2011, he'd be thanking me and crucifying the very same officers he's now charged with protecting. Making this case "go away" only harms the citizens and visitors to New York. People need to know that according to the loopholes of the laws of the City of New York, armed and uniformed police officers can have a front-row seat to an attempted murder (by a spree-killing fugitive they are searching for no less) and not only NOT move a muscle, also NOT be held accountable.

While I am not a lawyer, I am a clear thinking person. I realize that Corporation Counsel flooded their motion with these examples to fluff their case, even if some of these examples are "extreme" in their relation to my case. I am not naïve. I do not believe the police in any jurisdiction have an obligation to prevent every crime. That would be impossible. Nor am I a huge believer in these "orders of protection". To me, it is simply a piece of paper. It is impossible to assign an officer to every order of protection "just in case" something happens. Again, I understand that. This is why I am so confused as to Corporation Counsel's inclusion of several of these instances, other than to fluff up their case. To me, that would be similar to me bringing up "stop-and-frisk" in relation to this case.

The "Stop-And-Frisk" tactics employed by the New York City Police Department garnered a lot of attention, both positive and negative. Both the New York City Police Department and then Mayor Michael Bloomberg feverishly defended the program and argued that it lowered crime and had taken guns off the streets. The tactic is where police stop and question people they suspect of unlawful activity and frisk those they suspect are carrying weapons. This is a tactic based on appearance. The simple fact is Maksim Gelman, dressed like he was and acting irrationally like he was, was a perfect candidate for stop-and-frisk. The fact that Gelman was a wanted fugitive and he knocked on a door and identified himself as a cop and there were two uniformed and armed police officers behind that very same window and door is inexcusable. On one hand, the police are saying it's perfectly legal to "profile" individuals for the safety and well-being of the public, yet when officers of the same department take absolutely no action against a fugitive wanted for multiple murders that they are assigned specifically to locate and apprehend and in kind jeopardize the lives of innocent passengers, that also is permissible. How can this be?

After the arguments that you've just read, I attempted to put this case in simplest form, as a finisher in an attempt to prove that Howell and Taylor absolutely owed a duty to protect. If I may:

The facts of February 12th, 2011 cannot be denied and they are quite simple-

A-the New York City Police Department was notified that fugitive spree-killer Maksim Gelman was on the run in the subway system.

B-the New York City Police Department deployed several officers throughout the subway system to apprehend Maksim Gelman.

C-Officer Terrance Howell and Officer Tamara Taylor boarded the same #3 subway train that I did with the knowledge of the murders from the night before and for the sole purpose to locate and apprehend Maksim Gelman.

D-Officers Howell and Taylor were very well versed as to Maksim Gelman's history of violence and had no reason to believe he wouldn't attack again.

E-Maksim Gelman attempted to enter the engineer's compartment by demanding to be let in, going so far as to impersonate a police officer, unaware that Officers Howell and Taylor were on the other side of the window and door he was banging on.

F-Officer Howell refused entry to Maksim Gelman, the spree-killing fugitive he was on the train to apprehend, but did not take further action until after I subdued Gelman. Neither officer came out to investigate or apprehend Maksim Gelman even though his face was clear to them through the window of the door.

G-Both Officers Howell and Taylor did not come out to investigate when another passenger was tapping on the window and waving them out.

H-By failing to take police action, Officers Howell and Taylor put the lives of every single passenger on that subway in jeopardy.

By virtue of the facts above, Officer Howell and Officer Taylor absolutely and unequivocally did have a special relationship to every single person in that subway car, including myself. By failing to take police action, they knowingly left a murderer, the murderer they were specifically assigned to apprehend, to remain in an enclosed area without a definite route to safety, with the same public they are sworn to "protect and serve".

<u>Chapter Twenty-Eight</u>

I ended my opposition papers by shooting holes in the statement submitted by Officer Terrance Howell. Talk about revisionist history. This is either cringe-worthy or so laughable it makes me want to cry. The following is the conclusion of my hard work, my "exclamation point" so to speak:

There's an old saying, "you don't bring a knife to a gunfight". Well, on February 12th, 2011, all I had in MY "knife fight" was my body. I, Joseph J. Lozito, subdued Maksim Gelman. I , Joseph J. Lozito, have the wounds to prove it. <u>My wounds are consistent with wounds suffered by an individual taking down a person with a large knife.</u> I can prove that any way that it needs to be proven. I missed several weeks of work based on the injuries I sustained subduing Maksim Gellman. Your honor, I confess, I am not a ninja. If I were, I would have subdued Maksim Gelman like a ninja would have and not sustained any injuries and not missed any work. The fact is, I was left alone to subdue Maksim Gelman and I did the best I could. Unlike Officer Howell and unlike Officer Taylor, I was not armed. Unlike Officer Howell and unlike Officer Taylor, I was not on that train to apprehend Maksim Gelman. Unlike Officer Howell and unlike Officer Taylor, I did not outnumber Maksim Gelman 2 to 1. Unlike Officer Howell and unlike Officer Taylor, I did not have the element of surprise on my side. I did my best and it almost cost me my life. It almost widowed my wife and almost left Joseph Tyler and Dominic Anthony without a father.

Officer Howell testified before a Grand Jury that he *"was about to come out, but he thought Maksim Gelman had a gun, so he closed the door and stayed inside"*. I appreciate his honesty. However, this admission is in stark contrast to his sworn deposition taken on July 19th, 2012 where he states *"I came out of the motorman's booth and noticed Gelman had a knife in his hand which I verbally ordered him to drop. He refused to comply with my order. As a result, I used necessary force to take him down to the ground and physically removed and recovered the knife from his hand. Subsequently, I placed handcuffs on Gelman"*. Several things are incorrect about this sworn statement-

A-Maksim Gelman was never verbally ordered to drop anything.

B-Even if he was, he couldn't comply because he was too busy attacking me and being taken down by me.

C-Necessary force was indeed used that day, but it was not by Officer Howell.

D-The knife was actually removed from Gelman's hand by me and was recovered by Officer Howell's partner, Officer Taylor.

E-Officer Howell was eventually able to handcuff Maksim Gelman. This is true. However, it was after I subdued him and after Alfred Douglas assisted him.

I poured my heart and soul into these opposition papers. I experienced every emotion known to man while doing so. Having to relive the incident and then having to relive the cowardice shown by the officers was too much at times. I was hopeful that Judge Margaret Chan would see things my way. I was hoping she'd see what I'd come up and think to herself, *"you know, I really think this needs to be heard. There are just too many questions here. I can't in good conscience dismiss this case"*.

Corporation Counsel filed a quick reply to my response. Nothing noteworthy or earth-shattering in it. More of the same "no special relationship", "no duty to protect" type stuff. Now it was just time to sit back and wait while the wheels of justice did their part. Nothing more to do. Or was there?

Chapter Twenty-Nine

While I was playing the waiting game, hoping against all hope that Judge Chan would see things my way, an interesting judgment came down. It was an appeal and it has more to do with my case than any case cited in Corporation Counsel's motion to dismiss. In this case, we have two NYPD officers, a subway station, an assault and a City of New York employee who stood back, watched, and did nothing. Go on you say? OK, let's talk a little Filippo v. NYCTA and Jannet Velez v. The New York City Transit Authority, shall we?

Jannet Velez and Camille San Filippo are police officers who witnessed a man commit a criminal act and took police action (there's a nice change from two *other* officers I know). They chased the man and said pursuit ended in a subway station. They attempted to arrest the man, he resisted, they sustained injuries when an altercation ensued and now they were bringing a case against the Transit Authority. Why you ask? Surely most perps don't surrender without struggle. This must happen all the time? Here's the wrinkle-both officers were in plainclothes (not in uniform). When they entered the subway station, they displayed their badges and asked the station agent, Sean Corbin, to call for backup. Corbin was on duty and inside a locked token booth that was equipped with an Emergency Booth Communication System. All he had to do to call for help would have been to press a button or step on a pedal. He did neither, nor did he make any other attempt to get help for the officers. He just stood back and watched the fight from his booth. Hmmm.

The plaintiffs' concluded that Corbin's "failure to call for help constituted negligence which was a proximate cause of their injuries" and the Transit Authority (New York City) filed a motion to dismiss stating that Corbin was under no duty to call for any assistance to plaintiffs. Guess what? The case was dismissed. But....

That decision was reversed on April 30th, 2013 and San Filippo was awarded damages and the "matter was remanded as to plaintiff Jannet Velez for further proceedings pursuant to CPLR article 50-B". The Transit Authority was indeed held liable for damages. The plaintiffs were aided by the case of "Crosland v. New York City Tr. Auth". In that case, the Court of Appeals ruled that the "Transit Authority could be held liable for the negligent failure of its employees to summon aid as they watched a gang of thugs fatally assault a passenger". Interestingly enough, the court stated "watching someone being beaten from a vantage point offering both safety and the means to summon help without danger is within the narrow range of circumstances which could be found to be actionable". The trial court held that Corbin had no obligation because plaintiffs were police officers. This, apparently, was incorrect. The fact that the plaintiffs were police officers didn't make a difference, the Court found the NYCTA liable for Station Agent Corbin's lack of action.

When I read this, I was excited. Judge Chan already had both sides of the argument, but here was something that I was sure would turn the tide in my favor. Remember, all I'm trying to do is create doubt in her mind. All I need is for her to feel uneasy about dismissal. I thought this was my proverbial "cherry on top". A copy was mailed to Judge Chan and to Corporation Counsel and every day I'd come home and check the mailbox hoping for my letter with a court date. I was still stuck in the waiting game, but now I was more hopeful than ever.

Chapter Thirty

While I was waiting for Judge Chan to render her decision, I decided to take my case to the people. Social media is an amazing thing. I admit, I'm not one for technology. If you need verification, just check-out my flip-phone. Mock if you will, but I love that thing. I've never been one for Facebook. I do enjoy Twitter and wish I was on it when the attack happened as surely I'd have more followers than I do now thus having a broader audience. I also never realized the power of YouTube. Sure, I've viewed videos on there, but I guess since I'm not a frequent visitor, I never gave it much thought. I also started a petition asking for signatures demanding that Judge Chan not dismiss my case. My timing on that was not great and it turns out the petition was a non-factor.

Remember when I went to Gelman's sentencing and I mentioned my friend Bauzen? He had an idea. He was friends with a man named Luke Rudkowski. Luke is a staff journalist and videographer for an organization called "We Are Change" and he thought Luke would be a big help in bringing my story to the people. I was all for it. Through a series of e-mails and texts, it was set. He'd film me on the subway telling my side of the story. There would be a twist though. Luke would also interview random passengers and ask them what they thought the police would do if they witnessed a violent attack. Then they'd be asked if they were aware of the law that states that the police actually have no obligation to protect the public. This could be big.

I had never heard of "We Are Change". I'm not one for social issues, or at least I *wasn't.* I generally don't like to venture outside my little circle of family and close friends. Luke is a badass. So is Sierra Adamson. These two are amazing people. The risks they take are crazy and the lengths that some go to thwart their efforts is downright criminal. Luke has called me such things as "courageous", "brave" and "heroic" but do yourselves a favor, please research what Luke and Sierra have done with "We Are Change" and tell me if those adjectives aren't applicable to both of them. I won't lie and say I'm now "Mr. Activist", not by any stretch, but Luke, Sierra and Bauzen have really opened my eyes to a lot of things.

One night after work, Bauzen, Luke and Sierra met me at my job and we spent a few hours on the subway. Uptown and downtown we went, all the while I was telling my story while Luke was filming. Most people were curious and listened in. Some just watched and some couldn't care less. Some people asked and we told them and I believe one or two may have recognized me. I tend to be quite the chatterbox when I feel like I have a point to prove so they had plenty of footage. My favorite part of the night was when Luke would interview the passengers. Believe it or not, each one said they thought the police would, or at least they *hoped* they would intervene and EVERY SINGLE ONE OF THEM said they thought it was a police officer's DUTY and OBLIGATION to protect the public. See, it wasn't just me.....or *you!*

Once the editing process was done, Luke sent the video over to me and I was absolutely floored. It was awesome. It was uploaded to the "We Are Change" website and YouTube shortly thereafter. We received an amazing response and as of this writing, the video has been viewed almost 418,000 times. It has been rated by almost nine-thousand users with seventy-six giving it a "thumbs down". I'll take that percentage any day of the week. If you haven't checked it out, please do.

I also started the petition and a Facebook page, albeit too late in the game for either to help with the "process". The petition garnered a nice amount of signatures and the Facebook page was and still is viewed by many, but nothing came close to helping as much as the "We Are Change" video.

CHAPTER THIRTY-ONE

There's a saying in combat sports that goes "NEVER leave it in the hands of the judges". Basically, it means finish the fight. When you leave something up to someone else's interpretation, you just never know what's going to happen. Unfortunately, I didn't have such an option. I did everything I could do to get this case to trial but whether it did or not was solely up to one woman, Judge Margaret A. Chan.

The waiting wasn't the hardest part in this case. The knife to the head while stopping a spree-killer trumped that, but the waiting did suck. I try to always think positive. I thought I made a great case answering Corporation Counsel's motion and felt the reversal of the Filippo case would make a difference. I was getting ready for court in my mind. Just as I had prepared myself to face-off against Gelman in court, I was now mentally preparing myself to go one-on-one with Michael Gibek. Thinking about being on the stand gave me goosebumps. One can write whatever they want on paper, but when you're under pressure to prove a point, or in Gibek's case, a lie, who knows how one will react? I was ready and ready in a big way. I wanted at Howell, Taylor and Gibek in court. I planned on stealing the show. I planned on exacting revenge for every second that I had to wait. For every lie I had to endure. For every scripted untruth in Howell's testimony. I would absolutely let them know they were now in a fight. But alas, it was not to be.

On July 25th, I was working off-site. While the I.T. guy was setting up our second terminal and before we opened, I checked my e-mail. I had an e-mail from Ed who asked me to call him ASAP. I stopped for a second and took a deep breath. Ed and I really hadn't had much communication since I showed him my opposition papers, so the e-mail was somewhat of a surprise. I figured it had something to do with the case and, remaining positive, I was hoping for good news.

I sent Ed a text telling him I was about to start working and couldn't call, but wanted to know what was going on. He answered back quickly and his text read something to the effect of, "I'm sorry Joe, we thought this would happen, but the judge dismissed your case". I have to take a deep breath even typing that because it makes my blood boil!

I was pissed for many reasons. My first question was how did Ed know before me? The court was well aware that I was proceeding pro se and I was furious that they'd contact Ed instead of me. It was nothing against Ed mind you, I figured it was yet another slap in the face from the court. I asked Ed as much and he told me it wasn't the court who contacted him, it was a reporter from the New York Post. Judge Chan had made her decision a week prior, but it wasn't filed until earlier that day. Naturally I was furious that my case had been dismissed. I also felt helpless since I still had to do my job and didn't want to tell anybody until I had time to call Andrea. I wanted to tell her in person and that was still a few hours away. "Frustration" would be an understatement.

I did my job. Kept this bad news to myself. I didn't tell my box-office partner for the evening nor did I tell any fellow Lincoln Center employees. I finished up, settled my money, dropped it off at Avery Fisher Hall and was on my way home.

I spoke to Andrea, Joey and Dominic on my way home but again, I wanted to tell Andrea in person, so I didn't mention it. It was eerily familiar to the day I was laid-off from Fleer and spoke to Andrea and Joey on the phone right after getting the news. It's a horrible thing when you want to open up to the people who matter most but you can't. Unfortunately, really good news or really bad news should be delivered in person and I was at least another hour away from home.

When I got home, I told Andrea we needed to talk in private and I broke the news to her. She didn't take it well. She was angry and upset. Who could blame her? While I was trying to settle her down, the boys heard her and asked if they could come in. I explained to them what happened and told all three of them that I could and damn well planned on appealing. I told them that the fight wasn't over and I meant it!

Chapter Thirty-Two

After breaking the news to my family, I went online to a website where scans of court documents are available in pdf form hoping this decision would be available for viewing. The bottom line was the case was dismissed but I had to know why and I had to know as soon as possible. Fortunately it was there. I had to read it numerous times because while Chan ultimately dismissed my case, it seemed like she agreed with points in my opposition. Confused? Join the club.

Right away, the first paragraph made me angry. It contained the following sentences: *"Plaintiffs also mailed an unsolicited letter to this Court dated April 23, 2013. The letter was not considered by the court as the motion was fully submitted".* I was blown away. My friend Barbara Musco has worked in law for many years and she was the one who brought "Filippo vs NYCTA" to my attention. I had every right to submit that letter before a decision was made. The fact that Chan disregarded the letter and admitted as much is disgusting.

She then proceeds to rehash the series of events. It's correct for the most part, except when she gets the order wrong of a few key elements. *"The subway car slowly proceeded into the tunnel between 34th Street and 42nd Street and came to a stop between stations. At this point, Mr. Lozito had no interaction with the police officers nor Gelman. Gelman, who was in fact on board the same subway car, approached the closed motorman's booth and claimed that he was a police officer. Denied from entering, Gelman turned around and walked towards Mr. Lozito. Another passenger approached the motorman's booth and excitedly motioned for the officers to come out. Gelman randomly confronted Mr. Lozito without provocation."* Most of that is correct, except Gelman didn't approach me after he was denied entry. Her version makes it sound as if the assault happened immediately after he banged on the door. Indeed it did not. I'd say that's a key piece of information that is incorrect. You'd think in a ruling of this magnitude, the facts would be indisputable.

Here's another interesting nugget from Judge Chan in the very next paragraph: *Mr. Lozito heroically maneuvered the knife away from Gelman and subdued him on the subway floor.* Well thanks your honor, I appreciate you acknowledging what I did. How exactly did you manage to dismiss this again? *Mr. Lozito claimed the police officers did not emerge from the motorman's booth to apprehend Gelman until the attack on him was underway.* Question, had they emerged *before* the attack, how would an attack have happened?

Allow me to dissect the next paragraph. *"Officer Howell's recollection of the events described how he observed something made of metal in Gelman's hands when Gelman approached the motorman's booth".* So Howell admits he saw Gelman approach the motorman's booth. Howell also admits he observed something made of metal in Gelman's hands. So what he's saying is, Maksim Gelman, the spree-killing fugitive who *stabbed* three people with a *knife* approached the area where Howell was with something *metal. Metal?* Was he not able to guess that the metal object may be, I don't know, a knife? After all, that was Gelman's M.O. *"Officer Howell yelled "gun" and took cover in the motorman's booth".* So the cop with the weapons yelled gun and then took cover in the motormen's booth leaving every passenger in the car with a murderer? *"Officer Howell ordered Gelman to drop his weapon, an order that was ignored, and he proceeded to "physically remove and recover the knife from [Gelman's] hand."* So wait, did Howell order Gelman to drop his weapon from within the motormen's booth? No wonder the order was ignored. Gelman probably didn't hear him. Or, and this is a more likely scenario, the order was never given. Yeah, I'm going with that story. After all, I was there. Plus, as I've already stated, I was the one who removed the knife from Gelman's hands and

Howell's partner was the one who recovered it. *"Officer Howell placed Gelman in handcuffs"*. Now this I cannot argue. I am however still looking for anyone involved on the side of New York City to note *anything* that Alfred Douglas did. The fact is, Howell *couldn't* and *didn't* handcuff Gelman until Alfred assisted him. Not his *partner*, Alfred!

It gets better: *"Plaintiffs claimed that the officers negligently secured their own safety in the motorman's booth while observing the attack on Mr. Lozito"*. Didn't Chan just quote Howell saying he *"took cover in the motormen's booth"*? *"Plaintiffs also claimed the police officers were negligent in failing to recognize Gelman when they boarded the train and in failing to heed the warnings made by another passenger"*. Yes and no. I have *never* stated that the officers failed to recognize Gelman when they boarded the train. I've said hundreds of times that they failed to recognize Gelman when he banged on the door they were hiding behind and while looking through the window, claimed he was a police officer and demanded entry. Also, when another passenger attempts to get their attention, attempts to get them to come out and they don't, I'd say they failed to heed. I'd say that's *"failed to heed 101"*.

Her decision goes on to read *"The crimes against Mr. Lozito were made even more compelling by his own narrative provided in his opposition. Mr. Lozito's pro se opposition papers are thoughtful, eloquently written, and demonstrated his zest and love of life which propelled him to survive the attack by Gelman and defend himself. Mr. Lozito described in dramatic detail the blows and defensive maneuvers he used to disarm and take down Gelman. His statements ring true and appear highly credible"*. I like this paragraph. I worked my ass off on those opposition papers. I cannot tell you how many hours I put in. I don't have a law library or a staff at my disposal like Michael Gibek and Corporation Counsel. I have myself and my pc. I appreciate the compliments, especially the part where she says ***His statements ring true and appear highly credible.*** The problem is the next word. Don't type *"however"*, don't type *"however"*..... She goes on, *"However"*.....damn!!

"However, it is well settled that absent a special relationship, discretionary governmental functions such as the provision of police protection are immune from tort

liability" meaning, two cops can watch a spree-killing fugitive attack and almost kill another person, not do a damned thing and not be held liable. *"Despite even very sympathetic facts, public policy demands that a damaged plaintiff be able to identify the duty owed specifically to him or her, not a general duty to society at large"*. Again, silly me, I thought apprehending a murderer would help me *and* society at large. I also thought it was their job. *"The law is abundantly clear that no liability flows from negligence in the performance of a police function unless there is a special relationship."* I'll just let that sink in with you. *"Even giving Mr. Lozito every favorable inference (see Derdiarian v Felix Contr. Corp., 51 NY2d 308 [1987]), this court nonetheless is bound to grant the defendants' motion to dismiss; plaintiffs have failed to allege a prima facie case of negligence as these facts do not establish a special relationship"*. Is the court really bound by *anything?* Judgments are overturned all the time...."Filippo vs NYCTA" for example. Precedents are set all the time. I guess Judge Chan wasn't interested in making a difference in society. Shameful.

She then goes on to explain the criteria for establishing a special relationship. *"The elements of this 'special relationship' are: (1) an assumption by the municipality, through promises or actions, of an affirmative duty to act on behalf of the party who was injured"* Serve and protect...no? Ok, go on: *"(2) knowledge on the part of the municipality's agents that inaction could lead to harm"* Howell and Taylor were unaware that by not apprehending Gelman, this killer may very well try to harm other people? Even Barney Fife could figure that out! *"(3) some form of direct contact between the municipality's agents and the injured party"* well, I didn't introduce myself and ask if they would do their job "in the event of spree-killer", this is true; *and (4) that party's justifiable reliance on the municipality's affirmative undertaking"*. Wait...what? *"While plaintiffs pointed to the officers' close proximity to the attack and their perceived ability to prevent it, proximity does not create a special relationship. Mr. Lozito conceded that he had no communication or contact with the police officers before the attack took place. The first prong of the Cuffy elements was not met here. No direct promises of protection were made to Mr. Lozito nor were there direct actions taken to protect Mr. Lozito prior to the attack. Therefore, a special duty did not exist."*

I urge all of you to read and reread those requirements and please, make casual conversation with every officer you see because you know...*you never know!*

"Ultimately, this case must be dismissed as a matter of law (see id; Valdez v City of New York, 18 NY3d 69; Blackstock v Board of Educ. of the City of New York, 84 AD3d 524 [1 st Dept 201 I])". Again, I disagree. If this is the case, why do we have a Court of Appeals? *"The dismissal of this lawsuit does not lessen Mr. Lozito's bravery or the pain of his injuries. It merely provides a resolution to this litigation. Accordingly, the defendant's motion is granted and the complaint is dismissed"*. Thanks Mr. Lozito, you're a brave MFer and thanks for getting a murderer off the streets, but this court is about to rape you and we're doing it sans lube!

CHAPTER THIRTY-THREE

Heeding Ed's warning from our very first meeting, I've always kept his "this is going to be a very tough case to bring to trial" statement in the back of mind. There was a small part of me that held out hope we'd go to trial and yes, held out hope we'd win the case and a judgment. One person accused me of going after the "ghetto-lottery" which I found humorous. I think it's natural for anyone bringing a potential lawsuit to court to think about what they would do with the money and I'm no different. I may have had different plans than others trying to hit the "ghetto-lottery" though.

For the record, I had read two reports that stated dollar amounts I was asking for. One had me asking for one million dollars and the other had me asking for ten million dollars. Neither were accurate. Neither Ed nor I had ever stated a dollar amount. The reality is, we barely touched on the topic in any kind of serious discussions due to the expeditious nature in which Corporation Counsel wanted me out of their hair. Andrea and I had discussions about dollar amounts we'd listen to but that was between her and I. Not even Ed was aware of our discussions.

Had we won any type of significant financial award, I had a two-pronged plan. The first part was to go on a vacation. Not just any vacation, but a vacation I dubbed "the vacation of yes". We've never actually been able to afford a family vacation. Hell, Andrea and I didn't have a "real" honeymoon. Our current financial situation has my family in a similar situation to millions of other families and that's watching every penny. Because of that, my kids have gone without a lot that their peers haven't needed to. They've had to hear "no" more than a lot of kids and while I know they're disappointed at those times, they always handle it with dignity. This would have been my opportunity to say "yes" to everything on a vacation. It would really be a vacation for them. Probably a dream kids vacation where the word "no" did not exist. If that makes me a bad person, then guilty as charged. These two young men have earned it. I make no apologies for wanting that for them. It breaks my heart that such a trip may never come to fruition.

The other part of the plan was simple. The money gets put away for two very important reasons. Now I'm wondering if this is indeed a *three*-pronged plan. First, college for the boys. That's a no-brainer. Like most parents, I want my kids to make a difference in this world. College may be part of the journey for one or both of them. They should be able to attend a school that would bring out the best in them, not just one that we can "afford" with loans, grants or the best case scenario, scholarships.

The second reason is a bit more grim yet very real. The simple truth is, I think I've handled all of this, I mean every single part of this, as best as can be expected. I try. Every day I try to make the best of it. The fact is however that I'm terrified that one day something in my mind may snap and render me useless as a husband, as a father, as someone who can provide financially for my family. Every night when my head hits the pillow, I take stock of the day and thank God I made it through without incident. There is so much about the mind we do not understand so I feel my fear is legitimate although I'm always hopeful my fear never comes to fruition. In the oft-chance that it does however, I wanted to be prepared.

The best part of winning an award, even if it matched the defunct USFL's award in their lawsuit against the NFL years ago, would be vindication. The system worked. I had my day in court and the jury saw through the bullshit spewed by the other side and victory was attained by the good guys. It appears however that day will never come.

I had been preparing myself for the day the dreadful call would come. However, no such preparation would be needed should Judge Chan have come down on the side of good. It would have been justifiable and we'd have had a little celebration and then planned our all-out warfare to bring down the Evil-Empire. As Gerard Butler's character Clyde Shelton once said in "Law Abiding Citizen"; *"I'm gonna pull the whole thing down. I'm gonna bring the whole fuckin' diseased, corrupt temple down on your head. It's gonna be biblical."* I love that movie. I get goosebumps just thinking about all of Clyde's quotable lines.

The other option needed preparation. It was like a kick in the nuts but the fight wasn't over. I told Ed I'd take twenty-four hours to "grieve" and then I'd be in touch to discuss my options for appealing the heinous miscarriage of justice!

I called Ed a day later and he told me that appealing was definitely an option. I had two very real roadblocks. The first was that Ed took my case on contingency. Contingency means if I don't get an award, he doesn't get paid. I really respected Ed for that. The thing is, this appeal would be extremely difficult to win and as such, Ed couldn't take this on contingency. He warned me that I may run into similar rejections from other lawyers strictly based on what's involved and that contingency would be a tough sell. He was right. I contacted a few lawyers and most wouldn't even talk to me unless I ponied up some cash just for a place at the table. That wasn't an option. The second roadblock was indeed overturning this decision. Ed had explained how difficult it would be to win this case and now I'd be asking an attorney to take the decision and attempt to reverse it. The appeals process is in many ways more difficult than the original process.

As I suspected, I was unable to procure representation and starting coming to terms with the fact that justice may not only be blind but it plays favorites as well. I was satisfied with my effort. I went up against insurmountable odds and took my best shot. New York City was petrified to have me testify. Actually, maybe they were petrified to have their officers testify? Either makes sense as both would be case-killers for their side. I did all I could and knew that I could look my kids in the eyes and tell them I did my best.

I did a follow up video for "We Are Change" with Luke and Sierra basically breaking the news to everybody but also announcing in a general manner that I'd be writing a book. I was sad to have had to do this as when I watched it, it gave it sort of a finality. On the other hand, I was ready to move on. Not being a drunken reality television personality or some other form of sub-human, I didn't have publishing houses beating down my doors for my story. So I did what I've done with everything else regarding this entire situation, I moved forward alone.

I started gathering my thoughts for the book. Writing a little here and there. I was on my own time and I wanted this project to be perfect. I was certainly well into the moving on phase when I received an odd message from a Twitter name I had never seen before. The message said that the person wanted to talk with me about helping me with my appeal and wanted a few moments of my time. I ignored the first message out of cynicism. I received another and I was planning on making contact. Before I could though, a call came for me at my job and that was when a man named Lalit Jain walked into the picture.

Chapter Thirty-Four

Lalit asked if I had a lawyer to help with my appeal and I told him that I had recused Ed, hadn't been able to secure a lawyer on contingency and that I was ready to move on. He asked me if I'd meet with him before I threw in the towel to hear him out and listen to his strategy for reversing Judge Chan's decision. At this point, I figured I had nothing to lose so I agreed. We'd meet a few days later and before that, he'd e-mail me some information to tell me a little about himself and where he planned to take this.

When I started reading his notes, my jaw dropped. I can say without hesitation that I have never met anybody who thinks like Lalit. It's almost as if he's on a different plain of thinking. To be honest, it was a bit overwhelming but the parts that I could comprehend, I liked. I liked a lot. When we finally met, Lalit presented a strategy where we could reverse the decision and finally get my day in court. Of course he had to explain it to me a few times since half of it sounded Greek to me. Just to give you an example, Lalit is the guy in the movie with the ideas so outrageous, he's mocked and you figure "this guy is crazy" because you think there's no way this plan could work. By the end of the movie, of course it worked, he was right all along. I call him an "evil genius who uses his powers for good".

The difference between Lalit and every lawyer that I had been in touch with it is that Lalit is actually not a trial lawyer. He's actually a tax lawyer. This whole "justice" thing is a passion for him. It's not his job, it's his mission. Lalit isn't a litigator so he doesn't think like a litigator. He thinks so far outside of the box that you can't even tell where the box was to begin with! Going the traditional route with my case got me to this point. I was happy to mix it up a little and see where it went.

So far, he's helped me file my first motion to help the court reverse and correct its decision. Once again, the court ruled against me. Soon, I will file my second motion for a Declaratory Judgment as to the rights and other legal relations of the parties required by 100% settled law. In the words of Lalit; *"It will use correct admissible evidence by sound minds to become 100% credible to insure conclusive Justice with factual support to make lawbreakers pay for causing legal injuries. It is the commonsense philosophy of law to legally let all live in truth, insuring privacy, safety and security of all protecting all before, during, and after due process of law for State Confirmed Security. This is "Truthisprudence" (a word I created) to help the Court cremate Jurisprudence, studied and practiced by all lawyers to help courts make nullities, knowing that not vacating a nullity as void by a conclusive decision with factual support will still make them trespassers-in-law and the Court give grounds to deny a Declaratory Judgment as proof positive of still being a conscious-shocking 100% uncredible court far more lethal than a Kangaroo Court."*

He goes on *"It's the law. It means the law that a court makes in its discretion and thus confesses that to **make the law** means to **make the lie the law.** It misapplies laws made by legislatures. It makes **erroneous factual findings** to protect lawbreakers as "justice". It forces law enforcement officers to enforce its law called a case-law. That is why no one is above the **law** means no one is above the **lie** sold as the law because absolute immunity protecting courts from paying for adding damages to prior damages caused by lawbreakers will not protect anyone else to take the law in one's own hands to do the same. That is why you were told by all lawyers, including your prior lawyer representing you, that you had no case to begin with and he had no reply to give to the answer by the defendants. Our taxes pay for wages and benefits of our authorities with jobs secured for life. Police officially eyewitnessed your "slice and cut" and confessed not risking their own lives to protect you. It's the law that is 100%*

settled by the Supreme Court of the United States. It says, "I did have a case since day one to begin with, that this law is not even known, much less understood, by trial lawyers or litigators who make fools of clients with no discrimination between smart clients and stupid clients. BELIEVE IT OR NOT. THIS IS THE BOTTOM LINE OF EACH AND EVERY LEGAL SYSTEM REVEALING THE TRINITY: IN GOD WE TRUST, IN DEVIL WE BELIEVE, IN GOD WE WON'T."

Pretty intense, no? I told you, he's on a different level. He's the "evil-genius" who uses his powers for good! Emphasis on *genius!* Lalit always corrects me when I say "hope" in reference to my appeals. He has more confidence than I do. Lalit is confident in his work and his beliefs, as am I. I just have zero confidence in the "justice" system. It has screwed me more than once. I know it's not in place for me, or for you. I've learned hard lessons that the most unjust thing on earth is the "justice" system. If we are successful in overturning Judge Chan's decision (yes Lalit, I typed "if") it will be talked about for ages. My pessimism lies not with what we produce and send to the court, it lies with nobody in a position to make change having the guts to do so.

Rest assured, the battle rages on. New York City and Corporation Counsel should know by now that I fight until the end and I won't go quietly. This is not over and hopefully my second book will the success story about how the system was changed...a blueprint for future generations to learn from.

Spiro Vlantis
Keith Trimble
Joe Lozito

CHAPTER THIRTY-FIVE

So, what about now? What am I up to now? One of things I love doing is taking private lessons with the best striking coach on the planet. That man is Keith Trimble. If you're a fan of boxing, kickboxing or MMA, you should know Keith Trimble. Keith is one of four owners of Bellmore Kickboxing Academy here in Bellmore, Long Island along with Spiro Vlantis, Matt Berman and Chris Cardona. It's an old-school gym and Keith is an old-school, hard-core coach. The fighters Keith has trained or is currently training reads like a who's-who of combat-sports. That list includes Rodrigo Gracie, ISKA world heavyweight kickboxing champion Derek Panza, welterweight kickboxing champion Tim Lane, undefeated boxer Chris Algieri, and MMA superstars like Jay Hieron, Phil Baroni, Ryan LaFlare, Dennis Bermudez, Gian Villante & Costas Philippou. If you add me to that list, you know what you get? A lot of really tough guys...and me!

I consider Keith more than a coach, I consider him a good friend. Our friendship almost never happened due to an incident at an airport that Keith and I just cannot agree on. I'll let you decide for yourself.

I was at JFK airport waiting for a flight to Las Vegas to see Keith Jardine fight Luke Rockhold. It was early in the morning and I hadn't slept much the night before. I would imagine I wasn't looking my prettiest. I admit, whether I'm waiting for a bus, a train, a subway or a plane, I absolutely check out my surroundings and the people waiting. I did this before Gelman and I do it straight through today.

Nothing menacing, just looking things over. While I'm doing this, this guy who looks like he walked off the set of *"300"* walks by me and we make eye contact and that's it. I remember thinking to myself "I hope he's a good-guy because if he isn't, he could be a handful." That was it. No incident, nothing.

We fly to Vegas and I catch up with Keith Jardine and his coaches and the next thing I know, I'm in the fighter's meeting. For a fan, this was very cool. I just kept my mouth shut as this was serious business for the fighters and the coaches. I had my head down and when I looked up, I saw Gian Villante making eye contact with me. Like I said earlier, I met Gian when I did Ariel Helwani's show. I was surprised he remembered me. I went over to say hello and who is he sitting with, the barbarian from the airport! Gian introduced us and I extended my hand and Keith shook my hand and grunted. I chatted with Gian for a few more minutes and then went back to where I was. The next time I saw Gian, it was the following night and he was TKOing Trevor Smith in the first round! That was awesome. I did not see Keith Trimble again for the rest of the trip.

At some point, I decided I wanted to try my hand at kickboxing. I asked Gian and Ryan LaFlare where they did their striking and they both told me to go to Bellmore Kickboxing Academy and ask for Keith. I will admit, I was very intimidated going into that place. Like I said, it's hard-core. I met Frank at the desk and asked for Keith but he was in California for a fight. He gave me an e-mail address for Keith and we eventually made contact. I came back to the gym when he was there and when I walked in, I saw the berserker from the airport. Don't ask me why, but I didn't put two plus two together that Gian was recommending his coach from the fighter meeting.

My first few private lessons went well. I witnessed, let's call it the "tough-love" Keith dispensed to everyone. Keith and Spiro have mastered the "good-cop, bad-cop" thing. Spiro, with his boy-band looks is always smiling and having fun. Then there's Keith. He's all business...until you get to know him. The first few times, Keith wrapped my hands for me. I think it was the third or fourth time I asked and he said something to the effect of "how much longer am I going to have to wrap your fuckin' hands?" That was a great day! He finally ripped into me. I felt like I belonged!

Since the airport incident in my mind really was a non-incident, I had no idea it registered with Keith...until *he* brought it up. He casually slid it in to a conversation that I "mean-mugged" him at the airport. Now you just read the whole story of what happened but in fairness to Keith, I've asked him to tell you how he recalls the day. If you know Keith, you're going to laugh your ass off and say "yep, that's Keith!" Ready? Here goes.

"I was at JFK airport around 8 am leaving for Vegas. I was walking to the gate and as I approach my gate to sit down, I notice a large man with a goatee and a baseball hat staring at me. I notice he has a UFC bag so I think "oh boy, here is another tough guy wanna-be." As I walk by this guy, he's grilling me. I think to myself it's too early in the morning for this shit. I sit down with my business partner Spiro and say to him "look at the tough guy grilling us." I go to the bathroom and as I pass this gentlemen he once again stares at me. I figure he either likes me or is just an ass. If he says something then I'll do whatever, otherwise I'm not indulging in this nonsense. It's too early in morning."

Keith then went on to tell me about the fighter's meeting we both attended; *"At the fighter meeting, a meeting you didn't belong in by the way, I see the same tough guy in the room. I'm sitting by myself behind my fighter Gian Villante. Guy walks in bald head and tattoos. So now I'm thinking he really is a tough guy wanna-be. All of sudden he says hello and starts talking to my fighter. With that, Gian introduces us. I stay in my seat and shake his hand. I really have no intentions or care to know this person."* Finally, I asked Keith if he remembered me when I met him at the gym for the first time and he said *"yes I remembered you. I'm bad with names but I remember all faces. I was thinking 'what the fuck does this guy want?' Gian wasn't at the gym but I figured you were looking for him."*

Now ladies and gentlemen, you have heard both sides. If you don't know Keith Trimble, google him. He's a monster. He has a presence. If there was indeed a mean-mugging, it did not originate from yours truly. Since the subway incident, I have met a ton of professional fighters. I can honestly say that Keith is one of the baddest dudes I have ever met. He's also one of the coolest. I know by his testimony he comes off a little rough around the edges, but that's just him. He's actually a great guy and a terrific coach. As I said earlier, he's the best striking coach in the world and I honestly consider it a privilege to train with him. I love going to the gym and when Keith and Spiro are there together, it's always a good time. I love those guys and I know they love me back. I will always be grateful to Gian and Ryan for pointing me in the direction of Bellmore Kickboxing Academy. We just need to work on Keith's memory a little.

For the record, when Keith's lovely wife Trish was presented with both sides of the story, she sided with me...that's right, me!

With GLORY Sports International Board Member Ivan Farneti

CHAPTER THIRTY-SIX

Aside from training at Bellmore Kickboxing Academy, I'm doing other things to keep myself busy. My favorite thing is spending time with Andrea, Joey and Dominic. I absolutely love watching Joey and Dom take their Brazilian Jiu-Jitsu and Muay Thai classes. More than anything, just watching them grow up is the most miraculous thing I could ever do. Andrea and I are so fortunate to have such amazing children. I'll keep it at that as nobody wants to read a chapter where I go on and on about my children but I will say, I am truly blessed and I hope if you have children, you feel the same way about them.

Andrea and I are typical of a household where both parents work. We'd both agree that we don't get enough time together as a couple but we make it work. Quality over quantity. I hope one day our circumstances are different and we're able to spend more time together but make no mistake, waking up to her beautiful face is one of the highlights of my day every single day.

I'm still a rabid sports fan. As always, I'm predicting a World Series victory for my beloved Atlanta Braves. I love what's happening down there and one of my dreams is to make it down to Atlanta for a game or two. I was never able to attend a game in Fulton County Stadium and I'm hopeful to head south before the team departs for their new home in a few years. I'm also continuing my quest to collect as many Kyle Farnsworth game-used jersey's as I can. If you know of any, especially from the Cubs, Yankees, Pirates, or Mets, please let me know. I'm cautiously optimistic about the Buffalo Bills, as I am every off-season. I love the young talent they're assembling and I keep telling myself that one of these years things will all come together. As for the Islanders, I don't know what to think. I love the guys in the uniforms but have serious reservations about the guys in the suits, starting at the top. Things will be different soon anyway when the bolt Nassau County for Brooklyn. I still cannot believe that is a reality. Absolutely disgusting.

Combat sports still play a major role in my life. Through the generosity of Dana White, I'm still able to attend any UFC event that I can make it to. Mixed Martial Arts is so huge now and so mainstream you can always find a fight on some channel on television at any time of the day. I'm also happy to announce that professional kickboxing is making a resurgence in the U.S. in a HUGE way because of the Glory Sports International organization. Of course if you follow me on Twitter, you're already well aware of this! In my opinion, kickboxing is the most exciting martial art in mixed martial arts and I couldn't be happier with the growth Glory has had in their short existence. I am happy to help promote the organization, the events and the fighters. I would have been happy to do so from a distance but I'm humbled to say that many of the heads of Glory (I call them the "Kings") have taken a liking to me and I'm honored to call them friends. Starting with the boss, Pierre Andurand and continuing with Jim Byrne (yes, that Jim Byrne, formerly of the UFC), Bas Boon, Martijn de Jong, Sebatien Van Dus, Scott Rudmann, E (the man behind the curtain), and my pal and fellow Paesano Ivan Farneti, they have made me feel like family. If you haven't yet watched a Glory event, do yourself a favor and catch one. You will not be disappointed. Just prepare yourself to be reeled in!

Other than that, I will wait for my time to come in terms of "justice". If you'll indulge me just one more quote from Clyde Shelton, this time to Judge Laura Burch, that in my opinion sums up the alleged "Justice System"..... *"you all hang out in the same little club and every day you let madmen and murderers back on the street. You're too busy treating the law like it's a fucking assembly line. Do you have any idea what justice is? Whatever happened to right and wrong? Whatever happened to right and wrong? Whatever happened to the people? Whatever happened to justice?"* True justice may never be in the cards for me in terms of the "Justice System" but by you reading this book, by you heeding my words and my warnings, by soaking in everything I've had to say, by spreading the word.....I can say a small measure of justice has been served.

With Kyle Farnsworth. The jersey is autographed "To Joe, The Strong Shall Survive! Kyle Farnsworth"

ACKNOWLEDGEMENTS

I would like to acknowledge some people who have helped along the way in some way, shape or form. I pray to God I haven't left anyone out. I would like to thank Alice In Chains, Pierre Andurand, Atlanta Braves, Bad Boy, Badass of the Week, Holly Baratta, Ed Bassmaster, Vincent Bellaran, Bellmore Kickboxing Academy, Kathianne Boniello, Ricky Bonnet, Charlie Brenneman, Jim Byrne, Inspector Harry Callahan, Hector Castro, Ed Chakmakian, Don Cherry, RJ Clifford, Mike Constantino, Tara Cuccias, Eddie Cuello, Anthony Cumia, Caro Delgado, Detective David Mills, Dethrone Royalty, Barbara & Vinny DiLello, Nick Disalvo, Pat Dixon, E-book Formatting Fairies, Shoshanna Evers, Dean & Valarie Ewen, Ivan Farneti, Kyle Farnsworth, Kenny Feder, Joe Ferraro, Nadia Fischer, Future Legend, Jonathan Gantt, Thomas Geiger, Thomas Gerbasi, Samantha Gibson, Caroline Giglio, Glory Sports International, Godsmack, Ian Goldberg, Randy Gordon, Greg Guy, Kerry Gwydir, Reed and Laura Harris, Gregg Hughes, Lalit Jain, Jackie Jennings, Steve Keeley, Courtney Keenan, Jay Kelly, Allan & Marla Kilfoyle, Ron Kruck, Michele Kutner, Daniel Lacroix, Jack Lambert, Angela Lozito, Carl and Dorothy Lozito, Manumission Skin Care, Luis Marin, Steven Marx, Miguel Mendes, Brian McCann, Adrienne Midgley, Mark Miller, Chuck Mindenhall, Patrick Moriarity, Bill Mouzakitis, Dale Murphy, New York Islanders, Jim Norton, Bernadette Pender, Philadelphia Eagles, Philadelphia Flyers, Rosalie and Bob Picariello, "Rowdy" Roddy Piper, Kahleem Poole, Doreen Puco, Lt.

Pyle, Mauro Ranallo, Ranger Up, Andy Razzano, Marissa Rives, Joe Rizzo, Dan Robinson, Bas Rutten, Michael Ryan, Scott Rudmann, John Sallis, Eric Seemann, Matt Serra, Frank Shamrock, Joe Sheehan, Wanderlei Silva, Deb Singerman, Somerset Patriots, Detective William Somerset, Mike Straka, Tampa Bay Rays, Tapout, Chris Torres, Keith Trimble, Angela Troisi, Kyle Turley, Kurt Twining, Scott Twining, Dan Uggla, Ultimate Fighting Championship, Joseph Valtellini, Rick Vaughn, Spiro Vlantis, Wawa, Jesse Wellens, Rick Wenner, Dana White, Christopher Wiger, Lucas Wingard, and Lloyd Woodard.

ABOUT THE AUTHOR

I currently reside on Long Island with the three loves of my life; my wife Andrea and my boys Joseph and Dominic. You can follow me on Twitter at *@joe_lozito* or on Facebook on my Justice for Joe Lozito page.

Made in the USA
Middletown, DE
29 October 2023